The French Wars of Religion 1559–1598

SECOND EDITION

R.J. KNECHT

LONGMAN
LONGMAN AND NEW YORK

Addison Wesley Longman Limited
Edinburgh Gate
Harlow
Essex CM20 2JE
England
and Associated Companies throughout the world.

Published in the United States of America
by Longman Publishing, New York

First published 1989
Second edition 1996

ISBN 0 582 28533 X PPR

British Library Cataloguing-in-Publication Data

A catalogue record for this book is
available from the British Library

Library of Congress Cataloging-in-Publication Data

Knecht, R. J. (Robert Jean)
    The French wars of religion, 1559–1598 / R.J. Knecht. -- 2nd ed.
    p. cm. -- (Seminar studies in history)
    Includes bibliographical references and index.
    ISBN 0-582-28533-X
    1. France--History--Wars of the Huguenots, 1562–1598. 2. France-
-Church history--16th century. 3. Saint Bartholomew's Day, Massacre
of, France, 1572. I. Title. II. Series.
    DC111.K54 1996
    944'.029--dc20   95-33514
                                                         CIP

Set by 7 in 10/12 Sabon Roman
Produced through Longman Malaysia, PA

CONTENTS

To Maureen

EDITORIAL FOREWORD

Such is the pace of historical enquiry in the modern world that there is an ever-widening gap between the specialist article or monograph, incorporating the results of current research, and general surveys, which inevitably become out of date. *Seminar Studies in History* are designed to bridge this gap. The books are written by experts in their field who are not only familiar with the latest research but have often contributed to it. They are frequently revised, in order to take account of new information and interpretations. They provide a selection of documents to illustrate major themes and provoke discussion, and also a guide to further reading. Their aim is to clarify complex issues without over-simplifying them, and to stimulate readers into deepening their knowledge and understanding of major themes and topics.

ROGER LOCKYER

PREFACE TO THE SECOND EDITION

In revising this edition I have rewritten part of the chapter on the massacre of St Bartholomew so as to reflect recent research which has cast serious doubt on the traditional version of that event. I have also reorganised chapters 7 and 8 so as to relate the political ideas of the Huguenots and of the Catholic League more closely to the events from which they sprang.

R.J.K.

Birmingham, 1995

NOTE ON REFERENCING SYSTEM

Readers should note that numbers in square brackets [5] refer them to the corresponding entry in the Bibliography at the end of the book (specific page references are given in italics). A number in square brackets preceded by *Doc.* [*Doc. 5*] refers readers to the corresponding item in the Documents section which follows the main text. Words which are defined in the Glossary are asterisked on their first occurrence in the book.

ACKNOWLEDGEMENTS

The publishers would like to thank the following for permission to reproduce copyright material: Cambridge University Press for extracts from *Francogallia* by F. Hotman, edited by R. E. Giesey and J. H. M. Salmon, published in 1972; Editions Gallimard for extracts from *The Assassination of Henry IV* by R. Mousnier; (c) Droz S. A. for extracts from *Lettres Historiquers pour les annies 1556–94* by E. Pasquier, edited by D. Thickett and *Dialogue d'entre le Maheustre et le Manant* by F. Crome, edited by P. M. Ascole; Prentice-Hall Inc. for an extract from Constitutionalism and Resistance in the Sixteenth Century: Three Treatises pp. 110–112 published in 1969.

1. *France during the Wars of Religion*

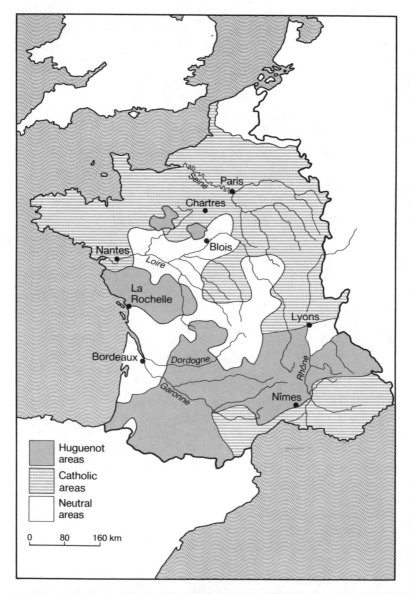

2. *Principal areas controlled by Huguenots and Catholics during the Wars of Religion*

PART ONE: THE BACKGROUND

1 THE GROWTH OF CALVINISM

THE EARLY FRENCH REFORMATION

Many people nowadays attach little importance to religion. Consequently, they find it difficult to believe that it played a major part in the civil wars that tore France apart in the late sixteenth century. They look for other reasons: political, economic and social. Religion, they argue, was merely a 'cloak' used by the great aristocratic families to give respectability to their ruthless pursuit of power. But the sixteenth century was not the twentieth: religion did rule the lives of thinking people; it offered them the hope of personal salvation in the next world. Even today religion can move people to action, as is daily demonstrated in the Middle East and India. But civil wars and revolutions are seldom the result of a single cause or grievance. Many interests are usually involved and the cross-currents can be bewilderingly complex. Material interests, including brutal power-hunger and greed, were certainly present in the French Wars of Religion, but religion was also crucially important.

The Wars of Religion are sometimes treated as if they were a self-contained phenomenon of the second half of the sixteenth century. They began officially in 1562, and historians have not always given themselves the trouble to look for causes further back than 1559. That, indeed, was an important year, when France and Spain signed the peace of Cateau-Cambrésis, bringing to an end the long series of Italian Wars. Both countries were virtually bankrupt, and the end of the war created an unemployment problem as many impoverished nobles had previously been employed in the fighting. The crisis was exacerbated by the accidental death of King Henry II in a tournament held to celebrate the peace. He left a widow, Catherine de' Medici, four sons and two daughters. The eldest son, Francis II, was only fifteen and was married to Mary, Queen of Scots, who belonged to the ultra-Catholic family of Guise. This family now gained control of the government, much to the disgust of the other two powerful aristocratic houses of Bourbon and Montmorency. Thus on top of a serious economic crisis, there was a build-up of faction. But this was not all. France had been for some time deeply disturbed by religious dissent. In fact, one of the reasons for the recent peace treaty was to give both sides a chance of dealing with the growing menace of heresy. To appreciate the role of religion in the overall crisis we need to look back beyond 1559.

It was during the reign of Francis I (1515–47) that Protestantism in the form of Lutheranism first entered France [90 *pp. 156–9*]. To many it seemed to answer a spiritual need. There was a spirit of evangelical reform in the air, keen to breathe a new inner life into a Catholic faith that had become largely a matter of idle theological speculation. In May 1519 a Swiss student in Paris reported that Luther's writings were being received 'with open arms'. The Sorbonne* or Faculty of Theology of the University of Paris did not condemn them until April 1521, so that they were able to circulate freely for more than a year. At first Francis I did not act very vigorously against Lutheranism. He was bound by his coronation oath to root out heresy in his kingdom, but in the early days of the Reformation heresy was not easily recognised or defined. It had much in common with the kind of evangelical humanism that had been tolerated in France for some time. The king was not prepared to accept any definition of heresy, not even the Sorbonne's, if it clashed with his personal inclinations and the encouragement he liked to give to the New Learning. His indecisiveness, whatever his reasons may have been, helped Lutheranism to take root in France. Warnings of its rapid diffusion were repeatedly made by the secular and ecclesiastical authorities. The 'contagion', as they liked to call it, did not spread from east to west, nor along the principal trade routes; it sprang up in disconnected places spontaneously and found support in most social groups. After 1530 it was found in almost every province.

Francis I's attempt to steer a middle course between reaction and reform ended abruptly in 1534 following the Affair of the Placards. On the night of 18 October Protestant placards or broadsheets were publicly displayed in a number of towns. One of them was even put up on the door of the king's bedchamber at Amboise. The affair was swiftly followed by an unprecedented wave of persecution, which the *Parlement** of Paris almost certainly instigated [170]. The repression was evidently a response to the message contained in the placards, which was a vitriolic attack on the Catholic doctrine of the Mass. The affair revealed how far French Protestantism had moved since its first appearance in 1519. For the placards were not Lutheran, but Zwinglian or Sacramentarian* in their uncompromising rejection of the Catholic doctrine of the Real Presence. In January 1535 a well-informed observer noted that all the people in France who were called 'Lutherans' were, in fact, Zwinglians (i.e. followers of the Swiss reformer, Ulrich Zwingli), an opinion endorsed four years later by Calvin. This re-orientation of dissent towards the Swiss Reformation is easily explained. Many Protestants had grown dissatisfied with Luther's moderation and looked to more radical reformers for leadership, although it is difficult to know how widespread Sacramentarianism had become in France. Switzerland had a stronger appeal to French dissenters than Germany because it offered them opportunities of writing and preaching in their own tongue. The shift of allegiance is well illustrated by the career of Guillaume Farel, a Frenchman who gave up Lutheranism for Zwinglianism in the early 1520s. He settled in Switzerland and turned the town of Neuchâtel into a base for an evangelical offensive against his own country. It was here that the placards of 1534 were written and printed.

The Affair of the Placards, it has been claimed, turned French Protestantism into 'a religion for rebels' [86 pp. 13–19]. This may be an exaggeration, but it certainly made the battle lines between orthodoxy and dissent much clearer. From 1534 onwards the attitude of the French monarchy to heresy hardened. Although the Edict of Coucy (July 1535) offered an amnesty to religious exiles, it specifically excluded Sacramentarians and even made the amnesty conditional on the recantation of beliefs previously held. From June 1540 onwards, when the Edict of Fontainebleau gave the *parlements* overall control of heresy cases, the flow of repressive legislation continued virtually without interruption. Meanwhile, the Sorbonne provided the persecutors with clear doctrinal guidelines, and in 1542 it drew up the first index of forbidden books. The last seven years of Francis I's reign saw a steep rise in the number of heresy prosecutions by the *Parlement* of Paris. Elsewhere the action of the *parlements* was uneven. In Dauphiné, Normandy and Guyenne they were lethargic, but in the south, where Roman law held sway, they were savage. Under Henry II (1547–59) the religious crisis in France gathered pace at an alarming rate. During the first three years of the reign more than 500 heretics were sentenced by the *Chambre ardente**, a special court set up within the *Parlement* of Paris. In July 1547 judges lost the right to vary punishments in heresy cases: henceforth death was to be the only penalty. Yet the repression did not check the progress of Protestantism. At first the congregations were left to look after themselves, but under Henry II they began to fall under the powerful influence of John Calvin.

JOHN CALVIN (1509–64)

The Reformation is often depicted as a single movement of revolt against the Catholic church begun by Luther and continued more effectively by Calvin. This is a simplification. Calvin did follow Luther in time, and did take over the leadership of the Protestant movement, but he was an independent figure whose contribution to the Reformation was personal and distinctive [110; 112; 129]. John Calvin was a Frenchman, born at Noyon in Picardy. As a youth he was sent to Paris to study theology, but in 1528 he took up legal studies at Orléans and Bourges. In 1531 he returned to Paris and devoted himself to the classics. His first published work was a commentary on a text by Seneca. It was probably in 1533 that Calvin was converted to Protestantism. In November his friend, Nicolas Cop, the rector of the university, preached a sermon which betrayed Lutheran sympathies. It caused an outcry and Cop fled to Switzerland. Calvin (who was at one time suspected of having written the sermon) retired to the south of France.

During the persecution that followed the Affair of the Placards Calvin fled to Basle, where in March 1536 he published the first edition of his *Institutes of the Christian Religion*. This contained a long preface, addressed to Francis I, in which Calvin defended his evangelical brethren against the vicious persecution that had been unleashed against them. He argued that they were the legitimate heirs of the early Christian church and denied that they had any seditious intentions. Although the *Institutes* were subsequently modified and enlarged, the original Latin edition contained the essence of Calvin's doctrine. It emphasised the majesty and absolute sovereignty of God and the hopeless corruption of man as a result of the Fall. Though predestination was implied, Calvin did not stress it at this stage. Another important aspect of his doctrine was the authority attached to Scripture, but he showed that reading the Bible was not enough: it had to be understood with the help of the Holy Spirit. Calvin had no time for subjective mysticism. Finally, while believing that the true church was invisible and made up of the elect of God (i.e. those predestined for salvation), Calvin believed in the necessity for a visible church, independent yet related to the state. In later years he devoted much time to the elaboration of the *Institutes*. The sixth and last edition of 1559 was five times larger than the first and differently arranged. The publication of the first French edition in 1541 did much to popularise the Reformation.

In 1536 Calvin returned to France to attend to some family business. He then planned to go to Strassburg, but the direct road was blocked by Imperial troops, so he made a detour to Geneva, expecting to stop there just one night. He found the city in the throes of a religious revolution led by Farel, who begged Calvin to stay and help him. Because of the strange set of circumstances that had brought him to Geneva, Calvin convinced himself that God wanted him to build a model Christian community there. The task proved difficult, as many of the leading citizens were moved by political rather than religious considerations. When Calvin and Farel tried to discipline them by the use of excommunication, they resisted and forced the reformers to leave. Calvin went to Strassburg, where he became minister to a congregation of French exiles. Under the influence of the local reformer, Martin Bucer, he developed his views of predestination and church organisation. Meanwhile, the situation in Geneva turned to chaos, and Calvin was invited back by his friends. He reappeared in the city in June 1541 and soon afterwards drew up a new constitution for the Genevan church – the *Ecclesiastical Ordinances*.

The chief innovation of the *Ordinances* was the recognition of the four offices of pastor, teacher, elder and deacon. The pastors, numbering five at first, constituted the 'Venerable Company': they were responsible for preaching the Gospel, administering the sacraments and admonishing members. The teachers had the duty of instructing the young in 'sound doctrine'. The twelve elders were laymen responsible for enforcing discipline; each supervised one of Geneva's districts and was expected to visit every family at least once a year. The deacons assisted the pastors in supervising poor relief, visiting the sick and the needy and administering the city's hospital. The core of the constitution of the Genevan church was the consistory, made up of the twelve elders and five pastors. It met once a week to admonish, reprimand and correct citizens who had opposed the official doctrine, stayed away from church or behaved in an unchristian way. The consistory could also excommunicate.

Geneva lay close to France's eastern border, and in the 1540s, as religious persecution intensified in France, numerous French Protestant exiles converged on the city. In 1559 the city council began to keep a register of refugees applying for the status of *habitant.* By 1560 almost 5,000 names had been recorded, but there may have been even more in reality [72 *p. 31*]. Such a huge immigration inevitably changed the face of Geneva. Accommodation and educational facilities had to be provided for the exiles. In 1559 the Genevan Academy was set up, partly to train those refugees who wished to enter the ministry. Its first rector was Théodore de Bèze, who eventually succeeded Calvin as leader of his movement. At Calvin's death in 1564 the Academy had 1,500 students. Another important development was the rapid growth of Geneva's printing industry. Between 1550 and 1564 it published over 500 titles (as compared with only 193 between 1540 and 1550). There were about 130 presses employing mainly French religious exiles. Their literary output was controlled by a small group of Calvinist zealots, including Jean Crespin, author of a famous martyrology.

THE CREATION OF A MILITANT CHURCH

The origins of the French Calvinist or Huguenot church are obscure. All that is known for certain is that here and there in France during the 1550s Protestants gathered in secret to worship. As yet they had no common confession of faith and no national organisation. Gradually, however, the influence of Geneva began to give shape to these scattered communities. In 1554 Calvin wrote to the faithful of Poitiers, advising them on how to set up or 'gather' a church [112 *pp. 152–3*]. He praised them for getting together to praise God and seek instruction, but warned them that the administration of the sacraments required the services of a suitable minister duly elected by themselves. They also had to ensure that the recipients of the sacraments were 'not still contaminated with papal superstitions'. In Paris the first Calvinist church was set up in September 1555 by the *sieur* de La Ferrière, a nobleman from Maine, who had come to the capital with his family to escape notice because of his religion. Soon afterwards his wife gave birth and he asked the faithful to have his child baptised, saying that it was impossible for him to go to Geneva. They allowed La Ferrière to administer the sacrament himself and this marked the beginning of the Parisian church.

A central direction, regarding both doctrine and church organisation, was urgently needed to give cohesion and discipline to the Huguenot communities in France, and Calvin's Geneva set about providing it. Between 1555 and 1562 it sent eighty-eight missionaries into France to help organise the new church. Many were Frenchmen who had gone to Geneva as religious exiles and had since been trained as pastors. The provenance of sixty-four is known: sixty-two were French by birth and almost every province, except Lorraine, was represented among them. Many came from Guyenne and Dauphiné. The social origins of forty-two missionaries are also known and they tell us something about the social distribution of French Calvinism: they included fourteen nobles (mostly younger sons), twenty-four bourgeois and four artisans. None came from the peasantry [87 *pp. 5–13*]. These statistics are consistent with what is known about the geographical and social distribution of early French Protestants in general [72 *pp. 42–62*]. Most of them were to be found south of the River Loire within a broad arc (the so-called 'Huguenot crescent') stretching from La Rochelle on the Atlantic coast to the valleys of Dauphiné in the east. North of the Loire, there were relatively few Protestants except in Normandy, where they were strongly represented [178]. Socially, the Calvinists were very mixed. Every social group and a bewildering variety of occupations were represented among them. But Calvinism was preponderantly an urban faith; it made relatively few converts among the peasantry.

How numerous were the Calvinists? It is impossible to give a precise figure, since only a few of their baptismal registers survive. In March 1562 Coligny allegedly prepared a list of 2,150 churches for presentation to the regent, Catherine de' Medici, but this was probably an inflated figure aimed at impressing her. A more realistic estimate puts the maximum number of churches at between 1,200 and 1,250 in the decade 1560–70. Some individual congregations were very large. Rouen, for instance, had 16,500 in 1565, but this was exceptional. It is unlikely that the total adult Protestant population exceeded 2 million or roughly 12 per cent of France's population. The French Huguenots were never more than a national minority [72 *pp. 42–3*].

The Calvinist missionaries underwent a rigorous training in Geneva [87 *pp. 14–29*]. They had to learn Latin, Greek and Hebrew so as to know their Bible really well. At first there was no formally organised training institution, so that Farel and Calvin themselves had to teach them, but in 1559 the Genevan Academy was able to take over this task. After completing their studies, the missionaries usually took up pastoral duties in Switzerland. This gave them useful experience: it attuned them to the strict, collective self-discipline of the Calvinist church. Before sending a pastor to France, the Venerable Company had to make sure of his fitness: he was made to expound a selected verse from Scripture at a meeting of the

Company. He also needed to be a good public speaker and his private life had to be above reproach. Once he had passed all these tests, he was given a letter accrediting him to a particular church in France. Missionaries were always allocated in response to a formal request from a local church. Thus the first missionary, Jacques l'Anglois, was sent because the faithful of Poitiers had asked for 'an upright man to administer to them the word of God' [87 *p. 32*]. Once a missionary had been assigned to a church, he prepared for his journey. He was usually accompanied by a representative of the local church acting as his guide. Some pastors came into France by little-known mountain tracks; others followed the principal trade routes disguised as merchants.

The main result of the activities of the Calvinist missionaries in France was the creation of a centralised organisation, consisting of local consistories, regional colloquies, provincial synods and a national synod, each covering a proportionately larger area. But this did not lessen the control exerted by Geneva on the affairs of the French reformed church. Calvin sent a personal representative to the first national synod held in Paris in May 1559, and he was mainly responsible for the Confession of Faith and Ecclesiastical Discipline drafted by that synod. In theory, one could appeal from the congregation to the colloquy, provincial synod and national synod in that order, but in practice, each church could appeal directly to Geneva.

The distribution of the Calvinist missions shows where the strength of the new faith was mainly to be found. The fact that more pastors were sent to certain towns than to whole provinces bears witness to Calvin's success among the urban middle classes. The main strength of his movement lay in towns like Poitiers and Orléans. Literally dozens of cities declared for the Huguenot leader, Condé, in 1562. At the provincial level Calvinism was strongest in Guyenne, Gascony, Dauphiné, Languedoc and Normandy. This can be explained in part by the fact that these areas were administered by Protestant lords, like Anthony of Bourbon or Admiral Coligny, or by men who were neutral. In north-east France, where the Guises or the Constable of Montmorency were all-powerful, the Calvinists made no headway. No missionaries were sent to Artois, Picardy, Lorraine or Burgundy, and only one to Champagne.

At first the Calvinist missionaries tried to operate as secretly as possible. Services were held in the homes of prominent Calvinists at night and in heavily curtained rooms. If houses were not available, barns or secluded spots in the woods were chosen. But sooner or later these meetings were bound to come to light. One of the earliest incidents took place in Paris in September 1557, when a group of Catholics tried to break up a Huguenot meeting in the rue St Jacques [87 *pp. 62–3;* 112 *pp. 154–5*]. Fighting broke out, 132 people were arrested and some burnings followed. This incident was important in giving the Huguenots unwelcome publicity. It also raised the question of how far they should resist persecution. Calvin told them that he sympathised with their plight, but that their only redress lay in prayer. It would be better, he wrote, for them all to perish than that the Gospel should be blamed for driving men to sedition.

Calvin did try to put pressure on the French king by seeking the co-operation of the German Protestant princes and of Anthony of Navarre, first prince of the blood. Tortuous negotiations took place in which an agent from Navarre called de Bury went to Germany and discussed a military alliance with the Count Palatine. This is the first indication we have of a possible resort to arms in France. De Bury was later arrested and all his papers seized, providing grist to the mill of those who believed that Calvinism was seditious. The German princes interceded with King Henry II in favour of the Huguenots, but he would not listen, calling them 'disturbers of the public peace and enemies of the tranquillity and union of Christians'. His opinion was not without foundation: between 1555 and 1562 there were many plots against the French government. Not all were planned by Calvinists, but all involved Geneva in some way. The best known was the Conspiracy of Amboise in March 1560 [*Doc. 1*] [87 *pp. 68–78;* 94; 117]. This was an attempt to seize the young king, Francis II, to get rid of his Guise ministers and put France under a Bourbon regent. The chief conspirator, La Renaudie, visited Geneva beforehand in the hope of winning the support of the Venerable Company. Calvin opposed the plot, if only because it was not led by Anthony of Bourbon, the only man in his view with any right to be regent. His opinion, however, was not shared by all the pastors. De Bèze allegedly gave secret encouragement to La Renaudie. Most of the Calvinist churches, however, preferred to follow Calvin's lead, which goes far to explain why the plot failed so dismally.

Whatever the truth may be concerning the Conspiracy of Amboise, there is no doubt that Calvinists soon became involved in politics. They took full advantage of the situation that followed the death of Francis II, when Catherine de' Medici showed a willingness to come to terms with them. More pastors were sent to France in

1561 than at any time previously; so many, in fact, that many Swiss pulpits were left empty. More pamphlets intended for French consumption were printed in Geneva than ever before. One of the most popular works was de Bèze's rhyming translation of the Psalms, which came to be used by Calvinist congregations all over France. They sang the Psalms so lustily that neighbours were often annoyed, and more than one secret worship location was discovered as a result. Some 27,400 copies of de Bèze's Psalms came off the Genevan hand presses towards the end of 1561 and early in 1562. The annual capacity of the Genevan printers may have been as much as 300,000 copies. Such a huge number of books, distributed far and wide, helps to explain the impact of Calvinist theology on Europe at large and on France in particular [87 *p. 100*].

During 1561 and 1562 nearly every Calvinist leader, except Calvin and Colladon, visited France: Farel went to Gap, Merlin to the house of Admiral Coligny, and de Bèze to the Colloquy of Poissy. For a time it looked as though Huguenots would take over the court itself. It became fashionable among courtiers to attend a Protestant sermon. In the south, Calvin's lieutenant Pierre Viret toured the cities: wherever he passed, Huguenots came into the open and provoked riots. Meanwhile, many lay exiles, including nobles, returned to France from Geneva on secret missions. In March 1560 the second national synod, held at Poitiers, prepared for political action at the next meeting of the Estates-General*: it drew up a memorandum casting doubt on the right of the Guises to serve as the king's advisers and appointed a group of representatives to work secretly at court. The Huguenots were no longer content to pray for release from persecution: they intended to put pressure on the king and his court. In 1561 they began sending agents to foreign powers.

In the light of all this evidence one cannot seriously doubt the importance of religion in the French civil wars. As H.G. Koenigsberger has shown, religion was the binding force which made possible the development of revolutionary parties of a distinctively modern kind [173]. Earlier oppositions had nearly always been limited to one social class or territorial unit. In the sixteenth century opposition movements became nationwide for the first time and included people from every social class ranging from princes of the blood to unemployed artisans. What brought all these elements together was religion. Only religion could unite the divergent interests of nobles, bourgeois and peasants over an area as large as France.

2 THE NOBILITY IN CRISIS

CALVINISM AND THE NOBILITY

Initially, Protestantism made its biggest impact on the lower orders of society. Thus Henry II was indignant when he learnt in 1558 that the aristocratic family of Châtillon had embraced the Protestant faith, which he regarded as the religion of humble folk. Writing about the French Protestants in 1561, the Venetian ambassador reported: 'Until now, because of the severity of the persecutions, one has seen only people of the lower orders, who apart from life had little to lose' [75 p. 85]. By the mid-sixteenth century, however, Calvinism had begun to make deep inroads into the nobility. One historian has estimated that half the French nobility went over to the new faith in the 1560s. A direct consequence of the conversion of many nobles to Calvinism around 1560 was the introduction of a military element into the opposition. The conventicles, which by now had come more into the open, became military cadres. Mass meetings of armed men protected by the local nobility and their retainers began to invade churches and to celebrate services openly in defiance of the public authority and the Catholic majority of the population. This did not only happen in the south: in July 1560 gatherings of about 4,000 Huguenots were reported from Rouen [30 p. 52]. The Huguenot military cadres were organised on a provincial and national basis in the same way as the religious communities had been formed into provincial and national synods. The synod of Clairac (November 1560) divided Guyenne into seven colloquies, each with its captain; that of St Foy [1561] chose two 'protectors', one for Toulouse, the other for Bordeaux [87 p. 109]. Under them were the colonels of the colloquies and the captains of the individual communities. When the first civil war broke out [1562] this organisation was more or less fully developed in Guyenne, Languedoc, Provence and Dauphiné, and in outline at least for the rest of France.

The relatively sudden conversion of so many nobles to the

Calvinist faith has been explained on economic grounds. The nobles, it has been suggested, were particularly hard hit by the steady rise in prices – the so-called Price Revolution – which affected western Europe generally in the sixteenth century. Their livelihood, it is alleged, depended on rents in cash that had been fixed by custom, and because, as nobles, they were debarred from trading or manual work, they were less able than other social groups to adapt to the new economic situation. What is more, they made their situation worse by living extravagantly: they spent lavishly on military equipment, on attendance at court and on various luxuries, such as clothes, jewels and buildings. As they incurred debts, they were driven to mortgage or sell their lands, which consequently fell into the hands of wealthy middle-class men from the towns. Finding themselves impoverished, the nobles attached themselves to the cause that seemed most likely to bring them easy profits [116, I *pp. 169–97*]. Calvinism offered scope for material gain at the expense of the Church.

Superficially attractive as this interpretation may be, it does not stand up to closer analysis. There were undoubtedly some impoverished noblemen in mid-sixteenth-century France, and there is plentiful evidence of investment in land by the urban middle classes. But there was no economic collapse of the nobility as a whole [50 *pp. 83–4*; 176]. The average nobleman was not dependent on fixed rents paid in cash: rents formed only a small part of his income and were often paid in kind. The basis of his wealth was land, which rose in value faster than prices. Nor was the nobleman completely debarred from profitable pursuits. He was allowed to graft and plant trees, and could manufacture glass and produce iron. Nor was he necessarily in attendance at court or in the king's armies. The *gentilhomme campagnard**, who managed his estates himself or with the help of bailiffs, was far more typical of the nobility in general than was the courtier or soldier [50 *p. 72*].

The day-to-day activities of the *gentilhomme campagnard* are described in detail in the diary of the sire de Gouberville, a petty nobleman from Normandy, who only went to court once in his life. The rest of his time was spent managing his estates and fighting lawsuits in defence of his interests. He kept his accounts very carefully and succeeded in making a profit from his farming, even in lean years [62]. Gouberville's diary is unique, but he was certainly not the only nobleman who coped well with the economic difficulties of the age. Recent research has demonstrated that in Beauce, Normandy, Béarn and Auvergne the nobility grew richer in the sixteenth century. In Auvergne, the average aristocratic income doubled in value between 1448 and 1551. In south-west France, the revenues of the king of Navarre went up sevenfold between 1530 and 1600, while the price of grain at Toulouse only trebled over the same period [*50 p. 84*].

A more likely explanation of the rapid diffusion of Calvinism among the nobility is clientage. A nobleman in sixteenth-century France was never an isolated figure: he had strong provincial and family loyalties. Although feudalism as a system implying military service had long since disappeared, the signs of feudal dependence – the fealty and homage sworn by a vassal to his lord – were still taken seriously [175]. Provincial feudalism survived in the form of patronage and clientage. Leaving aside royal patronage, the nobility was divided into local clientèles. No nobleman of middle rank could expect to be admitted to the court, the Church, the army or the administration, or to be promoted therein without the support of a patron. This was often a nobleman of greater substance to whom in childhood he had been attached as a page. La Noue tells us that a nobleman with an income of 700 or 800 *livres** per year and four or five children on his hands could only educate them by sending them to a wealthy neighbour as pages [*116, I p. 167*]. This would create an indebtedness in later life: the father and his sons would become the creatures of their benefactor and would follow him wherever he went, be it to court or to war. Thus it was that a nobleman who decided to become a Calvinist would carry with him into the new religion all his clients. This certainly happened in south-west France where the process of aristocratic conversion to Calvinism has been compared to the spreading of an oil stain. For example, the clientèle of the Gascon nobleman, Pons de Polignac *sire* des Roys, was 'a veritable religious spider's web'. It included many of the 500 people prosecuted for heresy by the *Parlement* of Toulouse in 1569 [*65 pp. 22–8*].

Calvin appreciated the impact of clientage on religious conversion. He attached great importance to winning over the nobility to his cause, knowing that the conversion of a single nobleman could lead to multiple conversions among his relatives and dependants. Théodore de Bèze, Calvin's principal lieutenant, was himself a nobleman, and therefore well equipped to appeal to his own class. He was sent to Nérac in 1560 and may have been responsible for the conversion of Jeanne d'Albret, the wife of Anthony of Bourbon and mother of the future Henry IV. A fair proportion of the religious exiles who went to Geneva were noblemen. They were indoctrinated alongside the pastors, so that in Geneva a close bond was formed between some of the future lay and ecclesiastical leaders of the Huguenot movement. Some of those who were trained as pastors returned to France and played a leading role in setting up Calvinist churches. In 1555 Louis, Prince of Condé, and his suite stopped in Geneva on their way home from a military campaign in Italy. They asked to hear a sermon and to visit the city. It is not known whether they met Calvin or any other Genevan pastors, but the visit shows that Condé was interested in Calvinism at an early date. His Protestantism may not have been entirely a matter of political convenience [87 *pp. 59–60*]. It is difficult for the historian to penetrate the religious conscience of any past figure. Some French noblemen of the sixteenth century may have become Calvinists out of adventurism or greed, but there were undoubtedly others who did so out of genuine religious conviction.

An important aspect of the mass conversion of the French nobility to Calvinism around 1560 was the role played by women [65 *pp. 47–49*; 187]. Already in the early part of the century Marguerite d'Angoulême, the sister of King Francis I, had given her encouragement and protection to evangelical scholars and preachers. Her influence had affected some of the ladies in her circle, who had to face the more serious challenges of the mid-century. They included Louise de Montmorency, the sister of the Constable and mother of Gaspard de Coligny, the future Admiral and leader of the Huguenot movement; Jacqueline de Longwy, duchess of Montpensier, who defended Huguenots at the court of Catherine de' Medici; and Michelle de Saubonne, ancestress of the Rohans, who led the Huguenots in the later civil wars. In the next generation Marguerite's daughter, Jeanne d'Albret, sponsored Calvinist preaching in Béarn and Navarre even before she announced her conversion in 1560 [114]. Other important Protestant ladies were Madeleine de Mailly, countess of Roye, whose daughter married and converted the Prince of Condé; Charlotte de Laval, the wife of Admiral Coligny; Françoise de Seninghen, mother of the Prince of Porcien; and Françoise du Bec-Crespin, mother of Philippe Du Plessis-Mornay, one of the leading spokesmen of the Huguenot cause [*Doc. 12*]. Perhaps half of the thirty-seven Huguenot women arrested for worshipping in the rue St Jacques in September 1557 may have been of noble birth.

Can it be that such women found self-fulfilment in the Calvinist faith? This has been suggested, but it is unlikely, for Calvinism was not better disposed towards female emancipation than was the

Catholic faith. In fact, women were given less personal responsibility in Calvin's Geneva than in Counter-Reformation Italy [53 *pp. 65–95*]. But noblewomen had more time to devote to religious pursuits and were probably more susceptible to the influence of a Protestant tutor to their children than were their menfolk. What is more, Calvin and his lieutenants appreciated the importance of winning noblewomen to their cause and kept up a lively correspondence with them. The favourable response of such ladies to the spiritual assault from Geneva probably owed a great deal to the influence of Marguerite d'Angoulême and her circle.

THE GROWTH OF FACTION

The last years of the reign of Francis I [1515–47] were marked by a considerable power struggle among the nobles who attended the court [90 *pp. 483–6*]. There were three main reasons for this state of affairs: the king's failing health, the enmity between his two sons, the Dauphin Henry, and Charles of Orléans, and the baneful influence of the king's mistress, the duchess of Étampes. The chief victim of the power struggle was the Constable, Anne de Montmorency, who was toppled in April 1541. But Henry remained loyal to him throughout his period of disgrace, while Charles became the darling of Madame d'Étampes, the Constable's implacable foe. Each prince became the focus of a court faction: while Montmorency's friends rallied round Henry, his enemies gathered round Charles. But the situation was completely changed by the premature death of Charles in September 1545. Less than two years later the king died, and the dauphin succeeded to the throne as Henry II. This released the forces of faction, which the old king had managed to some extent to contain. Madame d'Étampes was banished from court with ignominy and replaced as the dominant female by her arch-rival, Diane de Poitiers, Henry's middle-aged mistress, who proceeded to distribute favours to her friends and relatives as unscrupulously as her predecessor had done. At the same time Anne de Montmorency returned to power as Constable (the head of the army) and as Grand Master (the head of the court). His arrears of pay were settled and he recovered his governorship of Languedoc, while his brother, La Rochepot, was reappointed Governor of Paris and the Île-de-France. In July 1551 Montmorency was created a duke and a peer, an unprecedented elevation for a mere baron, placing him on a par with the highest in the land [115, I *pp. 34–45*].

Montmorency's power and wealth were enormous [54; 161]. He

owned large estates to the north of Paris, including the beautiful châteaux of Chantilly and Écouen, and also in many other parts of France. In addition to the revenues accruing from these lands, the Constable received an annual salary from the Crown of 25,000 *écus**, so that he was probably the richest man in the kingdom. By virtue of his high offices of state he ruled over the army and the court; he also chaired meetings of the king's council and directed foreign policy. He was renowned for his authoritarianism and orthodoxy in religion. Montmorency buttressed his wealth and authority with an extensive clientèle. He spared no effort in advancing the fortunes of his relatives of both sexes. His five sons took up military careers, while his daughters (except three who became nuns) married into blue-blooded families (Turenne, La Trémoille, Ventadour and Candale). Montmorency also helped his nephews, the three Châtillon brothers: Odet, Gaspard and François. Gaspard de Coligny and François became soldiers, and in 1552 Coligny was appointed Admiral of France (an essentially administrative office which did not entail sea-going) [123]. Odet went into the Church, becoming a cardinal at the age of sixteen. But he was an exception: few of Montmorency's male relatives went into the Church, and this proved a mistake, for it enabled the rival family of Guise to gain control of the upper clergy.

Historically, the most sinister aspect of the palace revolution that followed the accession of Henry II was the emergence of the house of Guise as a political force [49]. Claude, the first duke of Guise, belonged to the cadet branch of the ruling house of Lorraine, which at that time was a duchy situated outside the kingdom of France. The family claimed descent from the Emperor Charlemagne and, in the female line, from the house of Anjou that had once ruled the kingdom of Naples. Claude won his duchy as a result of his military services to Francis I. He was essentially a soldier, who never spent much time at court, but his brother, Jean, Cardinal of Lorraine, acquired fame as a distinguished patron of scholarship and the arts. Claude had several children by his wife, Antoinette de Bourbon, sister of the Constable of Bourbon, who had turned traitor. Among the children two achieved political pre-eminence in the reign of Henry II: the first was Francis, count of Aumale, who soon became a duke, and the other was Charles, Cardinal of Lorraine. Both were in the flower of manhood, intelligent and immensely ambitious. They also had the backing of Diane de Poitiers, who needed a counterweight to Montmorency's influence. Their sister, Mary, was the Regent of Scotland and mother of Mary, Queen of Scots.

The reign of Henry II is largely the story of the rivalry between the two houses of Montmorency and Guise. This found expression in the conduct of foreign affairs. Whereas Montmorency was in favour of peace between France and the Empire, the Guises had warlike ambitions, notably in Italy where they had certain interests by virtue of their Angevin ancestry. Two important marriages helped to promote Guise ambitions by linking them more closely to the Valois dynasty. In 1548 they cut across English designs in Scotland by carrying off their niece, Mary Stuart, and marrying her to the Dauphin Francis. Secondly, in December 1549, Francis, duke of Guise, married Anna d'Este, daughter of the duke of Ferrara and granddaughter of King Louis XII of France. In 1552 Henry II invaded the Holy Roman Empire, capturing Metz and occupying Lorraine. The Emperor Charles V retaliated by besieging Metz, but the duke of Guise put up such a stout defence that he was forced to retire, a humiliation which precipitated his decision to abdicate three years later. This event was soon followed by the truce of Vaucelles, which should have lasted five years. But it was soon broken, largely because of Pope Paul IV, who wanted French help in driving the Spaniards out of Italy. In 1556, after Spain had invaded the Papal States, Henry II sent Guise to Italy with an army, ostensibly to aid the pope, but in reality to conquer Naples. The duke, however, never got much further than Rome on account of events in France. In August 1557 a Spanish army commanded by the duke of Savoy invaded northern France from the Netherlands and laid siege to St Quentin. Montmorency marched to the relief of the town, but suffered a crushing defeat on 10 August. Six hundred French nobles were taken prisoner, including the Constable himself and four of his sons. A wave of panic swept through Paris, but St Quentin held out for seventeen days, long enough for the king to recall Guise from Italy. The duke was appointed *Lieutenant-Général** of the kingdom, and seeing that the Spaniards had already retired of their own accord, he decided to strike at their ally, England, by a surprise attack on Calais in midwinter. He captured it in only eight days and became a national hero overnight [182].

While Francis, duke of Guise, crowned his family name with laurels won in battle, his brothers Charles and Louis linked its fortunes irrevocably to the Catholic church. Charles's ecclesiastical career owed much to his uncle, Jean, Cardinal of Lorraine. He became archbishop of Rheims at fourteen and then Coadjutor of Metz. In July 1547 he was made a cardinal, and when his uncle died in 1550 he was able to add many of his benefices to those already in his possession. In the same year he was allowed by the pope to collate freely to all the benefices attached to his archdiocese and to many religious houses. This enabled him to build up an extensive ecclesiastical clientèle. For much of his career Charles was an arch-pluralist: altogether he collected some twenty-four abbeys, including Cluny and St Denis, the richest benefice in France, which was normally reserved for members of the royal family [140]. Charles's annual income has been estimated at the huge sum of 300,000 *livres*. In many respects Charles epitomised the ideal Renaissance prelate: he was intelligent, learned and cultivated, and his manners were unusually polished (unlike Montmorency who was notoriously gruff). But like many art patrons he was intensely avaricious: after the papal conclave of 1550 he carried away from Rome twenty-five crates filled with marble and bronze statues [115, I *p. 47*]. Like Diane de Poitiers, with whom he got on well, he grabbed the lands of ministers and courtiers who had fallen from grace in 1547. It was thus that he obtained the estates of Dampierre, Meudon and Marchais. His brother Louis was not in the same league politically, but he was no mean churchman. In the course of his career he held successively the sees of Troyes, Albi, Sens, Metz and Bordeaux, which he combined with some rich abbeys. His extensive ecclesiastical patronage effectively enlarged that of his brother, Charles, since it operated within the same family interest. In 1553 he too became a cardinal, so that the house of Guise could boast of having two cardinals of the same generation.

The Wars of Religion brought into conflict the three great families of Montmorency, Guise and Bourbon, but under Henry II the Bourbons were relatively insignificant. The power and wealth they had once enjoyed had been seriously diminished as a consequence of the treason of the Constable of Bourbon in the reign of Francis I. Under Henry II the head of the family was the Constable's nephew, Anthony of Bourbon, duke of Vendôme and governor of Picardy [128 *pp. 55–72*]. Being the direct descendant of Robert, sixth son of Louis IX, he was first prince of the blood (i.e. he was next in line to the throne after the sons of Henry II if they had no male heirs). In October 1548 he married Jeanne d'Albret, daughter of Henry, king of Navarre, and niece of King Francis I, and in 1555 he succeeded in her right to the throne of Navarre [114 *pp. 73, 106–19*]. At the same time he exchanged his governorship of Picardy for that of Guyenne and withdrew to Béarn. His younger brother, Louis, Prince of Condé, became responsible for the Bourbon clientèle north of the Loire without having the status necessary to the promotion of its interests at court. Anthony was widely regarded as a good soldier: otherwise his merits were few: he was ambitious, but shifty and dissolute. His chief purpose, to which he subordinated everything else including religion, was to recover that part of Navarre which had been lost to Spain in 1512 or to secure adequate compensation for it. This led him into treasonable dealings with Spain which lost him much credit in France.

3 THE CRISIS OF 1559–60

Two important marriages were arranged under the treaty of Cateau-Cambrésis: the first between Henry II's daughter, Elizabeth, and King Philip II of Spain; and the second between Henry's sister, Marguerite, and Emmanuel-Philibert, duke of Savoy.

As part of the double marriage celebrations a tournament lasting several days was staged in Paris. Among the participants was the king of France himself. On 30 June 1559 he was struck in the face by the lance of Gabriel de Montgomery, captain of the king's Scottish guard. Ten days later Henry died of his injury, leaving the throne to his fifteen-year-old son, Francis II [48 *pp. 589–93*]. In theory Francis was old enough to rule, but in practice he lacked the necessary maturity and experience. The government accordingly passed into the hands of his mother, Catherine de' Medici, who chose to rely heavily on Francis, duke of Guise, and his brother, Charles, Cardinal of Lorraine, the uncles of Francis's queen, Mary, who was also Queen of Scots.

The change of monarch was immediately followed by a reorganisation of government personnel. Diane de Poitiers, Henry II's mistress, was banished from court, François Olivier took over the chancellorship from Jean Bertrand, and Francis of Guise replaced Anne de Montmorency as Grand Master. But, significant as they were, these changes were accomplished without violence. Nor was Montmorency totally deprived of authority: he remained Constable of France and Governor of Languedoc. From his home at Chantilly he continued to dominate an extensive clientèle, well-endowed with offices. Apart from the Montmorencys, the most important rivals of the Guises were the Bourbons: Anthony, king of Navarre, and his brother Louis, Prince of Condé. As princes of the blood they were entitled to rule the kingdom during Francis II's incapacity. Both, however, were Protestants, and Anthony, the first prince of the blood, was in Guyenne when Henry II died and he took a very long time getting to court [128 *pp. 60–2*]. He was urged by some friends who met him at Vendôme in August to assume his rightful place at the head of the government. By the time he arrived at court, however, the Guises were firmly in control of affairs. A pretext was found for not giving Anthony accommodation at court, and while he was admitted to the king's council (*conseil privé*)* he was carefully excluded from the innermost council which decided policy. Anthony feebly acquiesced in this situation instead of making a stand. He even accepted an invitation to accompany Elizabeth of Valois to Spain in the hope of ingratiating himself with her husband, Philip II, and obtaining restitution of Spanish Navarre. As for Condé, he allowed himself to be sent on a mission to the Netherlands for the ratification of the recent peace treaty.

The most urgent task facing the Guise administration was to bring the royal finances into some kind of order. The public deficit exceeded 40 million *livres*, of which 19 million were owed immediately. Some public officials had been waiting as long as four years to be paid their wages. The Crown's revenue was reckoned at 12 million *livres*, but this was an optimistic figure, for there was much tax evasion. In an attempt to deal with this situation the government raised a forced loan: among the provinces Normandy alone was asked to contribute 800,000 *livres*. At the same time various curbs were placed on royal expenditure. Now that peace had been signed, a reduction of the military establishment was decreed. The settlement of wages to captains and soldiers was deferred. When a crowd of disbanded troops turned up at court and clamoured for their due, the Cardinal of Lorraine sent them packing under threat of hanging. They left angry and bent on revenge [101 *p. 20*].

In the religious sphere the change of monarch did not signal any change of royal policy. If anything, the savage persecution that had marked the last years of Henry II's rule was intensified. The Edict of Écouen was rigorously enforced. Police raids in Paris produced more arrests and on 23 December 1559 the *parlementaire** Anne du Bourg, who had voiced Protestant opinions, was burnt at the stake. More repressive legislation was also enacted: on 4 September 1559 the destruction of all houses used for illegal meetings was ordered, and on 9 November the death penalty was extended to anyone holding or attending such meetings. In February 1560 nobles who failed to enforce the new laws were threatened with the loss of their judicial rights [101 *pp. 21-2*].

All of this was, of course, supremely depressing to the Protestants, who had seen the hand of God at work in Henry II's accidental death and had hoped for some relief from their sufferings. They had looked to Catherine de' Medici, who was thought to be reasonably disposed towards them. The Paris church petitioned her to ensure that the new reign was not besmirched by innocent blood. In reply, she undertook to work for the improvement of their lot, provided they avoided gatherings and that 'each lived secretly and without scandal'. When this promise went unfulfilled, the Protestants warned Catherine that God would not allow the spilling of innocent blood to go unavenged: just as her husband had suffered punishment, so might she and her children feel God's wrath. Such impertinence merely exasperated Catherine and removed any inclination towards moderation that she may have previously felt [47 *139–40*].

What could the Protestants do to ward off the threat of extermination presented by the new régime? Could they risk offending God by taking up arms in self-defence? Was it not good Protestant theology to believe that 'the powers that be are ordained of God' and, therefore, that it is sinful to oppose them, however wicked they may be? Calvin's opinion on this matter, as expressed in his *Institutes of the Christian Religion*, seemed to offer little scope for resistance. 'Let no man', he wrote, 'deceive himself here. For since the magistrate cannot be resisted without God being resisted at the same time, even though it seems that an unarmed magistrate can be despised with impunity, still God is armed to avenge mightily this contempt towards himself.' Calvin would not even condone resistance to a tyrant. 'We are not only subject', he wrote, 'to the authority of princes who perform their office towards us uprightly and faithfully as they ought, but also to the authority of all who, by whatever means, have got control of affairs, even though they perform not a whit of the princes' office.' The reason for this is that 'they who rule unjustly and incompetently' have been set up by God 'to punish the wickedness of the people' [124, II *pp. 193–4*].

Did this mean that the French Protestants or Huguenots could not hope for any theoretical backing for resistance from their spiritual leaders? Not quite. Calvin was a master of equivocation and he occasionally dropped a hint that resistance might be possible in certain circumstances. In a letter to François Morel, pastor of the church in Paris (August 1560), Calvin did not rule out forceful resistance to the Guises, provided this was led by Anthony of Bourbon, first prince of the blood. But the latter, as we have seen, proved a broken reed. He was far more interested in regaining Spanish Navarre than in championing the Protestant cause. This left Condé as a possible leader of the Huguenots, and it seems that he was very soon involved in a plot to overthrow the Guises.

The origins of the so-called Tumult of Amboise are shrouded in obscurity. According to the historian Lucien Romier, the initiative was taken by Condé in August 1559 after he had despaired of his brother Anthony, but the evidence for this is inconclusive. A well-informed contemporary source, Régnier de la Planche, ascribes the initiative to an unspecified group of persons [*Doc. 1*]. Having agreed on the need to restore 'the ancient and lawful government of France', they consulted some French and German jurists, who advised that an armed coup against the Guises would be lawful if it was led by at least one prince of the blood. It may have been at this stage that Condé was approached. At his suggestion an indictment of the Guises was prepared and a plan drawn up to arrest them and make them account for their administration to the Estates-General. In late September 1559 Antoine de La Roche-Chandieu, a young Parisian pastor, travelled to Geneva to inform Calvin of the plot. But the latter advised against it, probably for practical rather than theoretical reasons [87 *p. 69*].

However, the momentum behind the conspiracy, fuelled as it was by widespread hatred of the Guises, was too strong to be checked even by Calvin's objections. Whatever may have been the role of Condé in the plot's early stages (he is often referred to as the *chef muet* or 'silent leader'), the responsibility of organising it was mainly shouldered by Jean du Barry, *seigneur** de La Renaudie, a petty nobleman from Périgord, who had embraced the Protestant faith in the course of an adventurous career. He was in Paris in September 1559 and for the next five months travelled extensively in France and Switzerland gathering supporters. These were for the most part impoverished noblemen. La Renaudie also hired mercenaries. He appears to have disposed of generous funds and it would be interesting to know their provenance. According to Romier, the plot was subsidised mainly by the English queen, Elizabeth, who wished to divert the Guises from sending military aid to the Scottish regent. Sir Nicholas Throckmorton and Sir Henry Killigrew were allegedly in league with the plotters, but the evidence for this is unsatisfactory [128 *pp. 97–112*].

In the course of his preparatory travels, La Renaudie visited Geneva. He made a bad impression on Calvin, but seems to have received encouragement from de Bèze, who gave him his own translation of Psalm 94 ('O Lord God, to whom vengeance belongeth, show thyself . . .') and promised to circulate an anti-Guise booklet, probably written by Hotman (see page 59), at the same time as the plot. Thus although the conspiracy was essentially aristocratic rather than Protestant, a measure of Genevan involvement may be taken as certain [87 *pp. 69–72*].

On 1 February 1560 La Renaudie and his followers held their final planning session at Nantes. The attendance was probably not as large as contemporary apologists have suggested. The purpose of the meeting was essentially to legitimise the plot. Thus it simulated the Estates-General, and La Renaudie made an opening speech pointing to the iniquities of the Guises. Loyalty to the king was emphasised and the aim of the plot was defined as the dismissal and trial of the Guises. La Renaudie was confirmed in his command and empowered to raise an army. The date of the coup was fixed for 10 March, though this was later put off for six days. From Nantes, La Renaudie went to Paris, where he stayed till the end of February. He sent out orders, found more recruits and dispatched arms, horses, supplies and cash to Orléans and Tours, where his troops – a motley assortment from various corners of France – were due to assemble. Secrecy, however, was not easily achieved in sixteenth-century France, and news of the plot soon reached the ears of the government from several quarters. Consequently, the Guises were able to pounce on the conspirators as they approached the royal residence at Amboise in small groups. Some, like La Renaudie, were killed in ambushes; others were interrogated and executed. Many were drowned in the Loire or hanged from the château's balconies.

The Guises claimed that the conspiracy had been aimed at the Crown. They set about implicating Condé and ascribed a share of the blame to 'some preachers of the new doctrine'. There was some truth in this charge: two Calvinist pastors – Chandieu and Boisnormand – were deeply implicated, yet the bulk of the reformed churches in France followed Calvin's lead. Thus the church at Nîmes refused to contribute any funds to the conspiracy, and apart from a few churches in Provence and elements in the Paris church, virtually none of the Calvinist congregations helped the conspirators [87 *p. 73*]. Contemporary Protestants blamed the plot's failure on spies and informers who had forewarned the Guises, but it can be argued that if the Protestants had lent their support more generally the conspirators would not have been defeated so easily. Calvin's influence was in large measure responsible for the plot's failure.

As for Condé, nothing positive was ever established against him. He may have been aware of the plot rather than a party to it, but he could not escape incrimination since he had a designated role to play in the plan to substitute the Bourbons for the Guises. After the plot had failed Condé swore in front of the court that he had played no part in it. He then retired to south-west France with his brother, the king of Navarre. Here they were joined by François Hotman from Strassburg and Théodore de Bèze from Geneva. What passed between them at Nérac in the summer of 1560 is anyone's guess. A new plot was certainly hatched at this time to capture the south-east provinces of France. This was taken furthest at Lyons, where the planning was elaborated by some young noblemen of Condé's suite, but the plot was soon foiled without much bloodshed [87 *p. 75*].

The aftermath of the Tumult of Amboise is surprising. One might have expected a wave of savage persecution aimed at the destruction of the Huguenots. Instead a policy of moderation in religious affairs was initiated. Indeed, it began even before the Tumult with the Edict of Amboise (2 March 1560). This granted a pardon to all the king's subjects for religious offences, provided they would live henceforth as 'good Catholics'. Only pastors and conspirators were exempted from this general amnesty [127 *pp. 347–8*]. A few days later, Francis II ordered the release of all religious prisoners and allowed dissenters to present to him petitions and remonstrances. The initiative for these acts of lenience can be attributed to the queen-mother, Catherine de' Medici [47 *p. 145*]. It is often supposed that she acted under the influence of the Chancellor, Michel de l'Hôpital, and Admiral Coligny, but this is not proven. L'Hôpital was absent from court between November 1559 and 20 May 1560, and only became chancellor on 30 June. As for Coligny, he was certainly sent to Normandy by Catherine and asked to report on the situation of Protestants in that province. What all this demonstrates is that the Guises, powerful as they were, could not overrule Catherine once she had decided to assert her authority.

The Edict of Amboise, as qualified by a circular of 31 March, explicitly maintained the existing ban on illicit assemblies and 'conventicles'. This created a problem for the Huguenots, who had now been given the right to petition the Crown collectively. How could they do this without conferring together? They got round the difficulty by interpreting the ban as applying only to seditious assemblies. In practice, the government tolerated private gatherings and hesitated in respect of public ones. In the words of Romier: 'uncertainty became a political system thanks to which the government could extend or restrict toleration without ever defining it precisely' [117 *p. 171*]. Consequently, there was much incoherence and diversity in the application of royal legislation, reflecting the private inclinations of the Crown's local agents. Unfortunately, Huguenots in various parts of France began to take advantage of the more liberal régime. They came out into the open, demonstrating their faith more or less provocatively, and in many places, especially in the Rhône valley, they attacked Catholic churches and religious houses. Such acts were frequently committed by turbulent nobles over the heads of the pastors.

A serious dilemma had been created for the authorities by the Edict of Amboise: were the Huguenots, who had been released from prison without being made to abjure, free to worship collectively? If not, how could they be made to conform, other than by a return to the régime of persecution which had failed so conspicuously? It was to sort out this dilemma that the government issued the Edict of Romorantin in May 1560 [127 *pp. 113–14, 349–51*]. This transferred the prosecution of heresy cases from the royal courts to the ecclesiastical tribunals. At the same time, the punishment of illicit assemblies and forceful demonstrations (i.e. seditious acts) was entrusted to the *Présidiaux**, the newest of the royal tribunals. The most important aspect of this edict was its preoccupation with law and order rather than religion. While clamping down severely on all acts of public disorder, it implied liberty of conscience and an end to religious persecution by the state. In practice, of course, religious dissent and sedition could not be so easily distinguished. The church courts proved incapable of dealing with heresy as it had now developed, and Huguenots resented the ban on collective action. The edict accordingly remained a dead letter.

Since attempts to bring law and order to the kingdom had failed, Francis II called a meeting of all his councillors to Fontainebleau on 20 August to devise some remedy for the current ills [117 *pp. 202–13*]. In addition to members of the *conseil privé*, the knights of the Order of St Michael were invited. One reason for the meeting and the special publicity it received was to rebut anti-government propaganda to the effect that the king was a minor at the mercy of his Guise uncles. Strenuous efforts were made to persuade the Bourbons to attend, but in the event they failed to turn up. However, Montmorency came, accompanied by his three Châtillon nephews and a large escort. On 23 August, Admiral Coligny presented two petitions – one to the king, the other to his mother – from the Protestants of Normandy, acting in the name of all their French co-religionists. Protesting their loyalty to the Crown, they asked for permission to have churches proportionate to their numbers in various places, where they might worship by day without fear of molestation [123 *pp. 39–43*]. There followed speeches by Jean de Monluc, bishop of Valence, and Charles de

Marillac, archbishop of Vienne. The former asked for a reform of the Church, starting with the papacy, while the latter endorsed this demand with the rider that reform would only succeed with the backing of a general church council or, failing that, a national one. Marillac also called for a meeting of the Estates-General. On 24 August Coligny made a speech deploring the fact that the king was hedged in by a guard of arquebusiers,* making it difficult for his subjects to petition him directly. He urged its removal and backed the call for a meeting of the Estates-General.

The main result of the Assembly of Fontainebleau was a decision to call the Estates-General for 10 December at Meaux and a national council of the Gallican church for a month later unless a preliminary agreement could be reached by the pope, the emperor and the princes regarding a general council of the entire Church. Meanwhile, civil unrest in many parts of France, but especially in Dauphiné and Provence, was beginning to assume alarming proportions. On 26 August, Jacques de La Sague, a messenger employed by Condé, was arrested, and on him were found papers which allegedly proved the existence of a vast plot. Under questioning La Sague incriminated the Bourbons and their closest dependants [117 *pp. 215–17*]. Whether or not the plot existed, the Guises reacted decisively: on 31 August Francis II ordered the king of Navarre to bring Condé to court. At the same time all the provincial governors, except Guise and Montmorency who remained with the king, were ordered to take up their stations, and a general mobilisation of troops got underway. On 2 October the venue of the forthcoming Estates-General was moved to Orléans, which was presumed to be the plotters' main base. A promise of military aid was also obtained from Philip II in the form of an armed threat to Navarre and Roussillon. Thus the Bourbons in Guyenne found themselves hemmed in by the king's army to the north and a Spanish one to the south. On 30 October, after many delays, the Bourbon princes arrived at Orléans, and Condé was promptly arrested and sent for trial. He refused to answer questions put to him by royal commissioners and asked to be tried by the whole *Parlement* and the peers of the realm. His demand was rejected, but on 5 December, before any further action could be taken against him, Francis II died.

4 CATHERINE DE' MEDICI AND THE COLLOQUY OF POISSY

The death of Francis II obliged the Guises to step down from their position of authority in the state, for his brother, Charles IX, who succeeded him was only ten years old, so that a regent had to be appointed. By custom the regency should have belonged to the first prince of the blood, Anthony of Navarre, but he had forfeited his position by his recent intrigues. Thus it was the queen-mother, Catherine de' Medici, who assumed the regency. She was forty-one years old and free of any compromising commitment to either the Bourbons or the Guises [47 *pp. 153–5*]. Her main wish was to preserve the independence of the throne, and in order to achieve this she strove to maintain a fine, if uneasy, balance between the two families, favouring each in turn. Because the Guises had dominated the realm in the recent past and still had a majority on the council, she turned first to the Bourbons to establish equilibrium.

In December 1560 the Estates-General assembled at Orléans, but they were reluctant to approve Catherine's regency, and were consequently prorogued. When they reassembled at Pontoise in 1561, they reflected the spirit of the new administration. The provincial estates*, meanwhile, displayed an aggressive anti-clericalism, called for the expulsion of the Guises from court, and even envisaged a Protestant France. Condé and Coligny were soon admitted to the king's council, and although Catherine was too politic to rout the Guises completely, she did vent her resentment of 'those who are accustomed to be king' in letters to her daugbter, the queen of Spain. Her feelings were formalised in a private agreement with Anthony of Navarre, wherein he waived his right to the regency and in return was appointed Lieutenant-General of the kingdom, an office only recently held by the duke of Guise [47 *p. 159*].

The advances made by the Huguenots at court were paralleled by their expansion in the kingdom at large. Feeling that the government was now on their side, Calvinist pastors shed all restraint. Popular passions were unleashed and the kingdom was torn apart by riots and disturbances, excesses being committed on both sides [118 *pp. 71–87*]. Catherine herself scandalised Catholic opinion by taking the king and her other children to a Calvinist sermon at the home of Admiral Coligny. The 'Huguenot Lent', as this period has been called, provoked a strong Catholic reaction [*Doc. 5*]. On Easter Sunday 1561 Anne de Montmorency, Francis of Guise and Jacques d'Albon, Marshal St-André, formed an alliance, known as the Triumvirate. They pledged themselves to defend the Catholic faith with the help of Philip II of Spain. The promoter of this alliance was François de Tournon, Cardinal-Archbishop of Lyons. The immediate aim of the Triumvirs was to win over Anthony of Bourbon to their side. He was to be seduced by means of compensation for Spanish Navarre, but Catherine, realising what was at stake, skilfully entertained Anthony with similar hopes. A prolonged contest for his allegiance ensued, which the Triumvirs eventually won, but not until February 1562 [128 *pp. 67–9*].

On 19 April Catherine published an edict which in effect granted the Huguenots toleration within their homes, but this was not enough to satisfy them. In a petition on 11 July they made several demands, including the right of public worship. In July a joint session of the royal council and *Parlement* of Paris banned all Protestant worship, while at the same time pardoning religious offences committed since the reign of Henry II. This edict satisfied no one and, not surprisingly, was never implemented. As Théodore de Bèze observed the chaos in France, he ominously reflected 'it looks like civil war or wretched servitude'.

One of three courses of action was open to Catherine. First, she could revert to a policy of outright persecution, but this had failed in the past and the Huguenots were now more numerous than ever. Secondly, she might win over the Huguenots, but that would mean confronting the Triumvirate with its military might, and unleashing civil war. Thirdly, she could try to heal the religious division by means of a national council or *colloquy* [128 *p. 114*]. In the end, it was this last course which she chose to pursue, with the support of a group of moderates that included Michel de l'Hôpital, Jean de Monluc, the Cardinal of Lorraine, and the king of Navarre. The foremost role must be given to Catherine. True, she was no theologian. According to the Venetian ambassador, she 'did not understand what the word dogma meant'. But her maternal instincts inclined her towards peace. She wanted national reform, provisional toleration and sweet reconciliation. 'Her irenicism may have been expedient, but it was nonetheless real' [106 *pp. 23–4*]. As for the

Chancellor, he had made his position clear in a stirring speech at the Estates-General of Orléans. 'Let us', he said, 'banish those devilish names – Lutheran, Huguenot, Papist – which breed only faction and sedition; let us retain only one name: "Christian" ' [*Doc. 2*].

The idea of a French national council was strongly resisted by Pope Pius IV, who held that a general council of the whole Church was the proper forum for the discussion of matters concerned with Christian unity. In fact, in November 1560 he had recalled the Council of Trent. But Catherine, while signifying her acceptance of this council, pressed on with her own plans. The Gallican church was ordered to assemble at Poissy on 20 July at the same time as the Estates-General at Pontoise. It was intended that the assembly would choose prelates to go to Trent and discuss their role, but the agenda also mentioned 'several things of great importance' about which Catherine wished to consult the prelates. This was clearly an oblique reference to the religious troubles in France. On 25 July she made it clear that the assembly was not to be restricted to prelates, but that 'all subjects' wishing to be heard would be welcome.

On 31 July 1561 Charles IX opened the synod of the Gallican church at the Dominican convent of Poissy, near St Germain-en-Laye, a favourite residence of the court. The synod was made up of prelates, canon lawyers and theologians. A majority of the prelates were rigidly orthodox, yet on 25 August all but five accepted the government's decision that the Huguenots should be given a hearing. Meanwhile, at Pontoise, the Estates-General put forward some very anti-clerical demands, which Catherine undoubtedly welcomed as a means of putting pressure in support of her own designs on the fathers gathered at Poissy. In return for a formal acceptance of her regency, Catherine issued the reforming Ordinance* of Orléans (31 January 1561) [119 *pp. 152–3*].

The Colloquy of Poissy began on 9 September 1561 [61; 106; 128 *pp. 113–37*]. It was attended by the royal family, the princes of the blood, the king's council, six cardinals, over forty archbishops and bishops, twelve theologians and many canon lawyers. For the Protestants, besides their party at court, there were twelve ministers assisted by some twenty laymen. The leader of the Protestant delegation was Théodore de Bèze, whom Geneva had sent in response to a royal invitation. He was a skilful diplomat, a polished orator, and, as a nobleman, he was well suited to dealing with court protocol. Though he was as firm in his faith as was Calvin he was more conciliatory in matters of form, and, at an early meeting with the Cardinal of Lorraine, offered up some hope of reaching an understanding. But a deep procedural gulf separated the two sides at the colloquy: while the Catholic prelates felt that the heretics were there to be instructed and judged, the Protestants came primarily to defend the principles of the Reformation within the colloquy and to proclaim the Gospel outside it.

The first full-length oration of the colloquy was delivered by de Bèze [*Doc. 3*]. After outlining beliefs that were shared by Catholics and Protestants, he turned inevitably to the differences between them and, in particular, to rival interpretations of the Eucharist. 'We say', he declared, 'that His body is as far removed from the bread and the wine as is heaven from earth.' This provoked cries of '*Blasphemavit!*' (he has blasphemed) from the prelates, who so far had listened in silence. An ambassador reported that 'the faces of all those who were within the hall changed colour, and it was remarked that even Coligny covered his eyes with his hands' [106 *p. 100*]. Yet the colloquy survived, and on 16 September the Cardinal of Lorraine replied for the Gallican church. His address was relatively accommodating in substance, though de Bèze was not impressed: 'never have I heard such impudence, such ineptitude . . .', he said, 'the old arguments a thousand times refuted . . . moved me to nausea.' A few days later, Ippolito d'Este, Cardinal of Ferrara, and Diego Lainez, General of the Society of Jesus, arrived as emissaries from Rome with the purpose of frustrating the colloquy.

On 22 September the government, responding to a petition from the Calvinists, decided to alter the form of the colloquy. Henceforth twelve Calvinists would meet as many Catholics in private conference. To placate the prelates the king would be absent, and, perhaps to encourage a more conciliatory atmosphere, most prelates would also stay away. But once again the Eucharist proved an overwhelming obstacle to conciliation. An attempt by the Cardinal of Lorraine to obtain the adherence of the Calvinists to the Confession of Augsburg* may have been a genuinely conciliatory gesture; on the other hand, it may have been a cunning ploy to divide the Protestant ranks [106 *pp. 125–8*]. Either way it failed, and an intemperate speech by Lainez attacking the legality of a national council further antagonised the Calvinists. Late in September the colloquy was again reconstituted by Catherine in a last effort to save it. This time five theologians from each side were appointed to confer on the Eucharist, but again they could not agree. On 13 October the assembly of prelates dissolved itself. Its results from Catherine's point of view were not wholly negative: the clergy had agreed to grant the Crown an annual subvention for six years in the first instance and a fairly comprehensive programme of reform for the Gallican church had been enunciated [130 *p. 123*]. But the regent's chief aim – conciliation between the Catholics and the Calvinists – had not been achieved.

De Bèze did not return to Geneva immediately after the colloquy. He continued to enjoy a splendid apostolate at court, while his fellow Calvinists preached freely in the kingdom at large. They scored a notable coup by converting Antonio Caracciolo, bishop of Troyes, to their faith. But zeal soon gave way to more aggressive feelings: churches were seized and fighting ensued. As both sides gathered arms, the Venetian ambassador reported that a 'great fear' was sweeping the kingdom. Yet Catherine continued to hope for conciliation. She now tried to achieve this by disciplinary concessions. On 24 October she applied to Rome for permission to sanction the taking of Communion in both kinds. Other concessions were urged by Jean de Monluc, Jean de St-Gelais and Cardinal Châtillon. But their demands were not well received in Italy, where the Council of Trent reopened on 18 January 1562 without a single French prelate in attendance. Meanwhile, Catherine summoned to St Germain deputies from the various *parlements* of the kingdom, carefully chosen from among those favourable to moderation. The result was the famous Edict of St Germain (17 January 1562) – commonly known as the Edict of January – which allowed the Huguenots to hold their assemblies throughout the countryside, but forbade them within walled towns [19 *pp. 8–14*; 127 *pp. 133–4, 354–6*]. This move, however, merely enraged the militant Catholics, and the *parlements* balked at registering the edict. Widespread street-fighting was narrowly averted in Paris. At the eleventh hour, Catherine, for reasons which are not clear, decided to hold another colloquy, this time at St Germain. A wide-ranging agenda, covering more than strictly disciplinary matters, was outlined by the Chancellor, but the debate never got beyond 'images', the first item on the agenda. The failure of this second colloquy sealed Catherine's disenchantment with theological debates. A few days afterwards she ordered a team of French bishops to set off for Trent. Now that a national council had failed, Catherine had no alternative but to pin her hopes of peace on a general one. But the fathers at Trent would accept conciliation only on their own terms; and, as a result of their deliberations, the gulf between Catholics and Protestants was widened, not bridged. The Colloquy of Poissy marked a watershed in the history of religious reform in the sixteenth century. Its failure marked 'the waning of moderation and irenicism, the breakdown of communication, the loss of contact, the hardening of religious frontiers, estrangement' [106 *p. 228*].

5 THE FIRST THREE RELIGIOUS WARS

The first three wars of religion were broadly similar in character: they were marked by the taking of arms, desultory military operations and unsatisfactory peace agreements, which allowed each side to prepare its revenge. Although the wars were fought on French soil, foreign powers became involved with them: while the Huguenots looked to England, the German Protestant princes and the Dutch rebels for military and financial help, the Catholics turned to the papacy, some of the Italian states and Spain. An early indication of foreign involvement was the meeting between the Guises and the duke of Württemberg at Saverne in February 1562. The Guises were anxious to prevent a coalition of German princes in support of Louis, Prince of Condé. Württemberg undertook to oppose such a coalition in return for a promise by the Guises to promote the Confession of Augsburg within France. It is unlikely that the Guises ever seriously intended to carry out this promise. At the same time, they managed to detach Anthony of Navarre from his brother, Condé. Anthony's wish to recover Spanish Navarre or to receive some adequate compensation for it has been described as 'the sole criterion of his political conduct, to which the claims of religion, the preservation of the monarchy and the tranquillity of France were all subordinated' [128 *p. 56*]. Papal and Spanish negotiators dangled various territories before his eyes, while the Guises drew him into their camp. As Lieutenant-General of the kingdom, Navarre commanded the royal army and shared a semblance of authority with the queen-mother, Catherine de' Medici.

On 1 March 1562 Francis, duke of Guise, returned from his meeting with the duke of Württemberg. He passed through the village of Vassy just as several hundred Huguenots were worshipping in a barn. Some of the duke's men tried to break up the meeting, but they were repulsed by the congregation. Guise's arquebusiers then opened fire on the Huguenots, causing heavy casualties [63, I *pp. 306–26*; 118 *pp. 318–21*]. Guise was accused by the Huguenots of starting the massacre, but he vehemently denied this. According to his version of the event, the violence erupted when the Huguenot worshippers pelted him and his men with stones. He claimed that he had even been struck in the face. The truth will never be known. What is certain is that the massacre was hailed as a victory by the duke's supporters in France. A triumphal reception awaited the Triumvirs (Guise, Montmorency and St André) in Paris on 15 March. Meanwhile, the Huguenots, now led by Condé, armed themselves. Fighting seemed likely to break out in the streets of Paris, yet Catherine continued to hope for a peaceful solution to the crisis. She appointed the Cardinal of Bourbon as Governor of Paris, thinking that he might prove acceptable to both sides. He tried to defuse the situation by persuading Guise and Condé to leave the capital, but his efforts were unavailing. At this stage Catherine leaned towards the Huguenots, and Condé should have gone to Fontainebleau, where she was residing, and carried her off along with her son, the king. Instead, he lost valuable time at Meaux, and allowed the Triumvirs to get to Fontainebleau first. Blaming the Huguenots for her plight, Catherine agreed under protest to return to the capital [47 *p. 171*].

THE FIRST WAR (1562–63)

On 2 April 1562 a group of Protestant nobles, led by Condé, seized the town of Orléans and their example was soon followed elsewhere [*Doc. 5*]. Within a short time the Huguenots had gained control of Angers, Tours and Blois. In the Rhône valley, the ferocious Baron des Adrets led an attack on Valence in which Guise's lieutenant was killed. Three days later, Lyons – the second city of the kingdom – fell to the Protestants. Alarmed at this turn of events, the Triumvirs allowed Catherine more scope in exercising her authority. She retired to Monceaux in May 1562 and negotiated with the Huguenots, albeit unsuccessfully. In the meantime, violence mounted on both sides, Huguenots being massacred at Sens (12 April) and at Tours (July) [*Doc. 4*]. A decree issued by the *Parlement* on 13 July authorised the slaughter of Protestants without risk of prosecution. According to the *Histoire ecclésiastique*, peasants and artisans suddenly turned into tigers and lions, while women took up arms alongside their menfolk. In areas controlled by the Huguenots priests and monks were killed and the churches sacked. Not even tombs escaped desecration at the hands of iconoclasts.

As the violence spread, Catherine looked for foreign help: she appealed to the pope, the duke of Savoy and Philip II of Spain. The Huguenots, for their part, turned to Elizabeth I of England. Religion apart, she had sound political reasons for responding to their appeal [128 *pp. 73–96*]. Her title to the English throne was being questioned by Mary, Queen of Scots, the niece of the duke and Cardinal of Guise. Elizabeth was also keen to regain Calais, which the peace of Cateau-Cambrésis had given to France for eight years, so she seized the chance to strike a hard bargain. On 20 September, at Hampton Court, Condé's envoys accepted her terms: in exchange for the port of Le Havre she promised them 100,000 crowns and 6,000 troops. Half the English troops were to be used to garrison Le Havre, which was to be exchanged for Calais, even before the eight years were up. But the treaty was a miscalculation by Elizabeth, as it greatly offended French national feeling, which was shared by Catholics and Huguenots [133].

The tide of war soon turned in favour of the Catholics, at least in the valley of the Loire, where they recaptured Blois. In Languedoc and Guyenne the Huguenots conquered some important towns, but they failed to capture Toulouse [155]. As a first step towards recapturing Orléans, the Triumvirs crossed the Loire from the north and seized Bourges (31 August), thereby severing Huguenot communications between Orléans and the south; but, when they learnt of the Protestant talks with England, they decided to recapture Rouen. It was in the course of this action that Anthony of Bourbon was fatally wounded (15 October). Rouen fell on 26 October. Meanwhile, the Huguenots holding Orléans were reinforced by 7,300 German mercenaries. They decided to march on Paris, but were held up by various sieges on the way, so that the duke of Guise was able to reach the capital first. The Huguenots then turned towards Normandy with the aim of linking up with the troops promised by England. They found their way barred at Dreux by the Constable, Montmorency. A battle was fought on 19 December which ended in a victory for Guise, who had come on the scene at the last moment [101 *p. 87*]. Montmorency and Condé were taken prisoner and St André was killed. This left Admiral Coligny and Francis of Guise at the head of their respective parties. Coligny left his brother, d'Andelot, in charge of Orléans and headed for Normandy, while Guise crossed the Loire and laid siege to Orléans.

On 18 February 1563 Guise was returning from a camp inspection when he was shot three times in the shoulder [128 *pp. 139–55*]. He died a few days later. His assassin was Poltrot de

Méré, a Huguenot gentleman from Saintonge. Under torture he implicated Coligny and other Protestant leaders in his crime. Later he cleared them, only to accuse them again. Coligny denied any part in the duke's murder, but he confessed to having rejoiced at the deed: 'I consider', he wrote to the queen-mother, 'this was the best thing that could happen to this kingdom and to the church of God, and especially to me and all my family and also, if Your Majesty permits me to say so, it will be the means to pacify the realm' [123 *p. 106*]. The Guise family, for its part, always believed in the Admiral's guilt and looked for revenge [*Doc. 6*]. It took the matter to law, and in January 1564 Charles IX evoked the suit to the *Grand Conseil**. He ordered its postponement for three years and forbade the parties concerned to take any action – legal or illegal – in the meantime. Two years later, at Moulins, the council declared Coligny innocent of the crime imputed to him, and Catherine obliged the Guises and the Châtillons to embrace each other, but the vendetta continued regardless [128 *pp. 157–61*]. The Guises could count on the support of all those Frenchmen for whom the murdered duke had been a national hero, the defender of Metz in 1552 and the conqueror of Calais in 1558. There is no doubt that the shots fired by Poltrot de Méré gravely exacerbated the civil divisions in France.

Catherine de' Medici was now rid of the principal leaders of the two rival camps. But Coligny was still fighting, Orléans was holding out, and, in Languedoc, Antoine de Crussol, who had been given the task of pacifying the province, seemed intent on carving out a principality for himself. Peace was urgently needed to check the formation of pockets of resistance or even of small Huguenot states within the kingdom. As negotiators, Catherine used the two chief prisoners of war: Montmorency and Condé. Ideally, Condé would have liked to see a return to the Edict of January, but his own freedom meant even more to him. So he agreed to the Peace of Amboise (19 March 1563), which guaranteed freedom of conscience, but regulated rights of worship in accordance with social status [19 *pp. 32–6*; 127 *pp. 142–4, 356–7*]. Noblemen with rights of high justice were granted complete freedom of Calvinist preaching and worship on their estates, while those with an inferior jurisdiction could worship within their homes. Protestant worship was allowed in towns held by the Huguenots before 7 March, and in one town in each *bailliage**. It was banned in Paris and its neighbourhood. Property confiscated from the Catholic church was to be restored. The peace was understandably criticised by many Huguenots.

Coligny accused Condé of having inflicted more damage on their churches than their enemies would have done in ten years. Calvin denounced the prince as 'a wretch who had betrayed God out of vanity'. But the treaty was not easily implemented. Catherine used all the power at her disposal, but she met with strong resistance from the *parlements*. In spite of their dissatisfaction with the treaty, the Huguenots helped the royal army to recapture Le Havre on 23 July. This was followed by an Anglo-French treaty (12 April 1564) in which Elizabeth ceded Calais to France in return for a cash indemnity.

On 17 August 1563 the majority of Charles IX was proclaimed before the *Parlement* of Rouen, and on 24 January 1564 the king and his mother set off on a progress that lasted for more than two years (till May 1566) and took them to many parts of the kingdom [37; 42]. It was intended to show the king to his subjects and to restore order among them by displaying his wealth and authority. In each *parlement* Charles declared his desire for peace, and, as he visited the border regions, he met some of France's neighbours. The most important meeting of this kind was at Bayonne in June 1565, where Catherine met her daughter Elizabeth, queen of Spain, and had talks with Philip II's chief minister, the duke of Alba [126 *pp. 35–46*]. From Catherine's point of view the purpose of the meeting was to arrange marriages between Philip's son, Don Carlos, and her daughter, Marguerite, and between Charles IX and the emperor's daughter. Spanish aims seem to have been the withdrawal of the French edicts of toleration and a joint campaign against heresy in France and the Netherlands. Protestants viewed the meeting with grave suspicion and later alleged that it had planned the Massacre of St Bartholomew (see below page 58), but this is unlikely. What the meeting actually achieved is unclear. Alba refused to commit Spain to the dynastic alliance proposed by Catherine and seems to have got nothing from her.

THE SECOND WAR (1567–68)

The worst Protestant fears about the Bayonne meeting seemed confirmed when Alba headed an army sent by Philip II to crush religious unrest in the Netherlands. His march along France's eastern border also alarmed the French government. When defensive measures were taken to protect France from a possible Spanish attack, the Huguenots saw them as a threat to themselves. Condé and Coligny left the court and a large Protestant army gathered near

Meaux. They planned to capture Catherine and the king, but the coup misfired. After escaping to Paris with her son, Catherine offered Condé an amnesty if he would lay down his arms, but he made impossible demands in return. So Catherine prepared for war. On 10 November, at St Denis near Paris, the royal army, led by the seventy-four-year-old Constable of Montmorency, defeated the Huguenots. However, Montmorency was fatally wounded and died on 12 November 1567 [54 *pp. 470–1*]. He was replaced as head of the army by the king's younger brother, Henry, duke of Anjou, who was only sixteen. He was given the title of Lieutenant-General.

Condé, in the meantime, met a German army under John Casimir of the Palatinate. They were joined by a Huguenot army from the south, which had made an epic march to the Loire, capturing Blois and relieving Orléans. Condé was strong enough to besiege Chartres in February 1568. By now Catherine badly needed peace, as her coffers were empty. On 23 March the Peace of Longjumeau was signed, bringing the second civil war to an end. It renewed the terms of the Peace of Amboise without any of its subsequent modifications [19 *pp. 53–8*; 127 *pp. 156–60, 358*]. No one regarded the peace as a lasting settlement. Catherine could not forgive the Huguenots for their attempted coup at Meaux. Whereas in the past she had favoured a policy of moderation, she now planned the destruction of French Protestantism. Alba had set her an example by executing Egmont and Hoorne, two leaders of the Dutch Revolt. Catherine told the Spanish ambassador that she hoped soon to imitate Alba's 'holy decision' in France. Another major blow to the Protestant cause occurred in July 1568, when Louis of Nassau, the brother of William of Orange, suffered a heavy defeat near Namur. By now the political situations in France and the Netherlands were interdependent. In August Orange made an alliance with Condé and Coligny. They accused their respective sovereigns of being misled by evil counsellors. The Huguenots doubtless had the Cardinal of Lorraine in mind, for he was the dominant influence in the French king's council. His known contacts with Spanish interests and his secret support for Catholic plots in England in favour of his niece, Mary, Queen of Scots, made him the arch-enemy of the Protestant cause.

THE THIRD WAR (1568–70)

The Cardinal of Lorraine was probably responsible for the secret order to arrest the Huguenot leaders which provoked the third civil war. Warned of the move, Condé and Coligny escaped from Noyers and after a hazardous journey that lasted four weeks they reached La Rochelle in mid-September. They were joined on the way by so many Huguenots with their chattels that Coligny compared their journey to the flight from Egypt of God's chosen people [101 *p. 123*]. On 28 September the Huguenot leaders were joined by Jeanne d'Albret, the widow of Anthony of Navarre, and her son, Henry. They brought with them substantial reinforcements. Condé now altered his strategy. Instead of operating from Orléans and the middle Loire, as he had done previously, he concentrated his main strength in the west, relying on a line of walled towns (Cognac, Angoulême, Montauban, Castres and Montpellier) to protect his lines of communication with the south. He also looked to a German army led by Wolfgang, duke of Zweibrücken, which entered France from Franche-Comté and, after overrunning Burgundy, established a bridgehead on the Loire at La Charité. Another army intended for Condé was intercepted and defeated by the duke of Montpensier as it marched north from south-east France.

On 12 March 1569 Henry of Anjou, who commanded the king's army in western France, met Condé's army at Jarnac [45 *pp. 113–18*]. In the battle that ensued, Condé, whose leg had been broken, was murdered in cold blood by one of Anjou's captains. The command of the Huguenot forces passed nominally to Henry, king of Navarre, but he was still very young, so Condé's effective successor was Admiral Coligny, who soon made his junction with Zweibrücken's army. From late June until September Coligny besieged Henry, third duke of Guise, in Poitiers. King Charles's army, in the meantime, received reinforcements sent by the pope, Florence and Spain. By late June it comprised about 8,000 horse and 16,000 foot. The strength of the Huguenot army was roughly the same, though it probably had more infantry. In July Coligny made overtures to the king. The civil war in France, he suggested, was a Spanish plot to draw French attention away from the Netherlands. In addition to demanding the free exercise of the Calvinist faith in France, he suggested a French invasion of Flanders as a means of reuniting Frenchmen in pursuit of a patriotic cause. But Charles IX said that he would only receive the Huguenots if they laid down their arms. On 12 July the *Parlement* declared the post of Admiral vacant and, early in August, confiscated all the property of the Huguenot leaders, depriving them at the same time of their offices. In September Coligny was condemned by the *Parlement* and a reward of 50,000 *écus* offered for his head [123 *pp. 131–5*].

On 3 October Anjou defeated Coligny at the battle of Moncontour in Poitou. But the Admiral managed to retreat towards the south-east and eventually regained the military initiative. While the king's army sat down to a long and costly siege at St Jean d'Angély (16 October–2 December), Coligny regrouped his forces, a move that has been described as 'one of the greatest achievements in Coligny's military career' [123 *p. 135*]. Having wintered at Montauban, he marched on Paris in the hope of securing a speedy and advantageous peace. The Huguenots, it seemed, were invincible. On 29 July 1570, therefore, peace was signed at St Germain-en-Laye. The edict of pacification of 8 August has been called 'a Calvinist charter' [19 *pp. 69–81*; 127 *pp. 175–77, 358–60*]. This is an exaggeration: Protestantism was still banned at court and in Paris. But the edict marked a distinct advance on its predecessors, for Protestants were granted security towns (La Rochelle, Montauban, La Charité and Cognac) for two years. They were allowed freedom of conscience throughout the kingdom and of worship where it had been permitted before the war; in the suburbs of two towns per *gouvernement** and in the homes of nobles with rights of high justice. Huguenots were also to be admitted to all universities, schools and hospitals; they were to have their own cemeteries, and were given certain judicial privileges to defend them against prejudiced judgments by the *parlements*. All confiscated property and offices were to be handed back.

6   THE MASSACRE OF ST BARTHOLOMEW

The Peace of St Germain and the fall of the Guises cleared the way for a reconciliation between the Crown and the Huguenots. Two important marriages were planned to facilitate this reconciliation: the first, between the king's sister, Marguerite de Valois, and the young Huguenot leader, Henry of Navarre, and the second, between the king's brother, Henry of Anjou, and Elizabeth I of England. But Catherine de' Medici's enthusiasm for these marriages was not shared by all the parties involved. Among the Huguenots, there was little support for the Navarre marriage: Jeanne d'Albret, Henry of Navarre's mother, was not sure that it represented his best interests, while Admiral Coligny opposed it [114 *p. 359*]. He would have preferred a marriage between Navarre and Elizabeth of England, but she saw no advantage to herself in such an arrangement. As for the Anjou marriage, it met with unexpected resistance from the duke himself: he thought he would be dishonoured by marrying a woman who was regarded as a bastard by the Catholic world [45 *pp. 141–8*].

While Catherine actively pursued her matrimonial schemes in 1571, the idea of a French military intervention in the Netherlands was being strongly promoted in France. William of Orange, the leader of the Dutch rebels against Spain, had left France after the siege of Poitiers (1569) in order to prepare an invasion of the Netherlands. But his brother, Louis of Nassau, and many Dutch exiles stayed behind. They organised raids on Spanish shipping from their base at La Rochelle, and with Huguenot help they prepared an attack by land on the Netherlands which would coincide with William's invasion. Such an expedition, however, needed the support of the French government, and its promoters set about winning over King Charles IX. He had so far shown more interest in hunting than affairs of state, but he resented the military reputation gained by his brother, Anjou, during the third civil war, and was attracted to the idea of conquering a part of the

Netherlands while Philip II of Spain was tied down by a serious Morisco revolt in the old kingdom of Granada. The negotiations for an Anglo-French marriage that were currently taking place also opened up the possibility of English co-operation in a Dutch enterprise. On 19 July 1571 Charles IX attended a secret meeting at the château of Lumigny, which was soon followed by another at Fontainebleau. Nassau attended the second meeting and possibly the first as well. The result of these meetings was a plan to partition the Netherlands between France, England and the Empire [126 *pp. 168–9*]. In assuming England's co-operation the plan anticipated a successful outcome of the Anglo-French marriage talks. But Anjou ensured their collapse by insisting on the exercise of his Catholic faith in England, a condition wholly unacceptable to Elizabeth and her ministers.

Admiral Coligny favoured a war on Spain in the Netherlands, and it was mainly on that account that he was persuaded in August 1571 to return to court. He was warmly welcomed by the king at Blois on 12 September, admitted to the king's council and given 150,000 *livres* as well as a lucrative abbey [123 *p. 147*]. However, the Admiral's position was less secure than these expressions of royal favour seemed to indicate. The king was trying to break free from his mother's tutelage, but her influence remained decisive. She not only distrusted Coligny, but also opposed his warlike designs on Spain. On the other hand, she needed his support for the Valois–Navarre marriage, viewing it as the keystone of a religious reconciliation in France. At first, Coligny opposed the match, fearing that it might lead to Henry of Navarre's abjuration; later he accepted it as the prerequisite to a war with Spain. The king's weakness and Catherine's distrust were not the only difficulties facing Coligny. To most Frenchmen he was a rebel and a heretic, and the Guises (with Spanish backing) looked for any chance of ruining him. In November it was reported that they were gathering funds and followers in Paris. The Huguenots countered this move by collecting round Coligny at Châtillon. France seemed once again on the brink of civil war, but the danger was narrowly averted. In March 1572 Charles IX again cleared Coligny of any guilt for the murder of Francis of Guise, but the vendetta was not so easily suppressed. Only the Admiral's blood could satisfy the Guises.

By 8 October 1571 Charles IX had given his approval to an armed intervention by France in the Netherlands, but his mother got the decision rescinded. News of the Spanish victory over the Turks at Lepanto (7 October) confirmed her in her reluctance to go to war with Philip II. Even so, Nassau and the other Dutch exiles in France intensified their preparations for an armed attack on the Netherlands. On 1 April 1572 the Dutch 'Sea Beggars'* captured Brill, and on 14 April William of Orange issued what amounted to a declaration of war on Spain. Nassau pressed Charles IX to join in, but the king felt unable to counter the wishes of his mother and of all his councillors, save Coligny. So Nassau acted alone: about the end of May he and some Huguenot confederates captured the towns of Valenciennes and Mons. Coligny again urged war on the king, but on 7 June Charles forbade his subjects to cross the Dutch frontier in support of Nassau. In mid-July a Huguenot nobleman, called Genlis, defied the ban by leading an army to the Netherlands, only to be routed by the Spaniards near Mons. Some two hundred men, including Genlis, were taken prisoner, while the rest were either killed on the field or butchered afterwards by peasants [47 *p. 281*]. News of the defeat caused wild rejoicing among the Parisian Catholics. Rumour had it that Charles IX had authorised the expedition, but he denied this on 21 July while affirming his friendship with Spain.

The Genlis affair made it all the more necessary for Coligny to intervene in the Netherlands in support of the Prince of Orange. He still enjoyed the king's favour and informed Orange that he would soon come to his aid. After a brief visit to Châtillon in late July, Coligny returned to Paris to promote his war plan, trusting in the king's continued favour and Huguenot support. He pointed to the dangers that would face France if Orange were defeated, and also to the restlessness of his own followers. According to Tavannes, the Admiral said that he could no longer restrain them and that the choice facing Charles IX lay between war with Spain and civil war. But Coligny still faced the resolute opposition of Catherine, who not only opposed war with Spain but also deeply resented Coligny's favour with the king. She feared that if the Admiral got his way nothing would prevent him achieving supreme power at her expense. The papal legate Salviati shared this opinion: France, he believed, would fall under the domination of the Huguenot party if she went to war with Spain. On 9 and 10 August the king's council decided in favour of peace. Yet soon afterwards 3,000 Huguenots assembled near Mons and the duke of Alba demanded an explanation. Coligny also gathered an army of 12,000 arquebusiers and 2,000 horsemen. Catherine viewed these developments with alarm and, in league with the Guises, may have decided to get rid of Coligny [47 *p. 283*].

In the meantime, negotiations for the Valois–Navarre marriage moved towards a happy conclusion. On 2 March 1572 Jeanne d'Albret, who had so far resisted Catherine's invitation to visit the court, arrived at Blois. She despised the court's pleasure-loving ways and resented her future daughter-in-law's refusal to convert to Calvinism, yet the marriage contract was signed on 11 March. Jeanne, however, was not to see the outcome: she died in Paris on 9 June. It was said later that she had been poisoned, but there is no evidence for this [114 *pp. 370–94*]. In spite of her death, preparations for her son's wedding continued, though time was lost waiting for a papal dispensation for a mixed marriage, which neither Pius V nor his successor, Gregory XIII, seemed ready to concede. The atmosphere in Paris became highly charged as numerous Huguenot noblemen converged on the capital, carrying arms and wearing distinctively austere clothes. The Guises also came with their large clientèle and took up residence at the Hôtel de Guise and in houses belonging to the clergy. At the same time fanatical preachers urged the Parisians to win salvation by slaughtering the heretics. Most of the preachers were Franciscan friars, but one of the most inflammatory was Simon Vigor. He prophesied torrents of blood if the wedding took place, 'for God will not suffer this execrable coupling' [68 *p. 65*]. Wild talk of this kind was in tune with a surge of popular discontent, which was in part provoked by a rise in the cost of food (a *setier** of wheat cost 5.75 *livres* in August 1569 and 8.58 *livres* in August 1572), but more probably by the favourable terms conceded to the Huguenots in the Peace of St Germain. Having lost the war, they were strutting about Paris as if they were the victors.

THE MASSACRES

The massacre of St Bartholomew's day has traditionally been interpreted as a unique event in the history of the Wars of Religion, for which the government of Charles IX has been blamed. Yet, as recent studies have underlined, it can only be explained satisfactorily if it is seen as the culmination of a long series of popular disturbances in Paris. Huguenots had been violently abused by Catholics for years. A particularly dramatic incident occurred in January 1569 when Philippe and Richard Gastines were arrested on a charge of holding a Protestant service in their house. Their arrest prompted a riot in which fifty people were allegedly killed. In July, the Gastines were hanged, their property confiscated and their house demolished. On the site, a stone pyramid surmounted by a cross was erected to symbolise the triumph of orthodoxy. When the Edict of St Germain ordered the destruction of all such monuments, the Parisians refused to obey. Eventually, the cross had to be forcibly removed to the Cemetery of the Innocents. Even so, there were more disturbances. The *Parlement* blamed the rioting on poor people. Historians have also looked for *agents provocateurs* – perhaps Spain or the Guises. But, if such agents were involved, they 'merely took advantage of already long-festering hatreds and encouraged their expression' [*57 p. 88*].

Not all the grievances of Parisians were religious: some were economic. The effects of war, bad harvests and high prices were causing much hardship. Yet, following the Peace of St Germain, Charles IX asked for 600,000 *livres* from the Parisians with which to pay off the mercenaries who had come to help the Huguenots. The Parisians said that they could not afford to pay this sum. In the end, the king had to be satisfied with half the amount, but even this proved difficult to collect. He also resorted to fiscal expedients. Wealthy citizens were coerced into buying *rentes**. Under the Peace of St Germain, offices which had been taken from Huguenots were to be returned to their former owners. Since the Crown had no money, Catholics, who were thus dispossessed, could expect little or no compensation. Similarly, those who had occupied Huguenot homes were now expected to hand them back. The potent combination of religious and economic grievances alienated Parisians from the government. They were prepared to forgive Charles IX on account of his youth, but they blamed his mother, who, they believed, held the reins of power. As an Italian, she could expect no sympathy from a fiercely xenophobic population.

On his return to court (September 1571), Coligny had been given a handsome pension and readmitted to the king's council. Parisians naturally concluded that he was exercising an undue influence on the young king. Sutherland has suggested that this was not so: Charles, it seems, resisted Coligny's advice. The Admiral, moreover, spent only five weeks at court between September 1571 and August 1572. His influence, therefore, cannot have been as great as historians have generally assumed [*126 pp. 315–16*]. However, the perception of contemporaries may have been different: noting that the Guises left court as Coligny returned, and that Charles IX was insisting on the strict enforcement of the Peace of St Germain, they drew their own conclusion. It was also Coligny who demanded the removal of the cross of Gastines. The news that the king's sister was about to marry the Huguenot prince of Navarre increased suspicion that the Protestants controlled the court. When a Huguenot army, led by Nassau, captured Valenciennes and Mons in May 1572, the rumours seemed confirmed. Charles IX, it was alleged, had secretly backed the enterprise.

On 18 August the wedding of Henry of Navarre and Marguerite de Valois was celebrated at Notre-Dame [70 *p. 52*]. It was followed by four days of festivities in the form of tournaments, banquets, balls and ballets. Their glitter contrasted sharply with the poverty affecting many Parisians. On 22 August, as Coligny was walking from the Louvre to his residence in the rue de Béthisy, he was wounded by a shot fired from the window of a house nearby. The assailant managed to evade capture by the Admiral's escort. His identity is uncertain, but he was probably Charles, *seigneur* de Maurevert. Historians have usually regarded him as a royal agent, but he may have acted on his own account. However, the house from which the shot was fired belonged to the Guises [35; 52 *pp. 462–68*]. As news of the attempted assassination spread through Paris, Huguenot nobles gathered at the bedside of their stricken leader. Later, the king himself came, accompanied by his mother and several courtiers. He promised to avenge the crime. A judicial enquiry, held on 23 August, implicated the duke of Guise. The city authorities, meanwhile, took steps to restrain the Parisians who were keen to express their hatred of Protestants. The Admiral chose to stay put in spite of the dangerous environment. At his request, the king gave him a bodyguard of fifty arquebusiers.

The attack on Coligny is unlikely to have been the opening shot of an attack on Huguenots generally. Had it succeeded, it would have been a tactical blunder, for the Admiral's followers would have been alerted to the danger facing them: they would have left Paris and started a new civil war. The plot having misfired, Coligny refused to leave the capital and placed his trust in the king's promise to track down and punish the would-be assassin. What happened next is unclear. According to Tavannes, the king and his council, meeting in the Louvre on 23 August, decided that civil war had become inevitable and that 'it was better to win a battle in Paris, where all the leaders were, than to risk it in the field and fall into a dangerous and uncertain war'. But Tavannes's memoirs were written by his son long after the events described and need, therefore, to be used with caution. All that is certain is that Catholics feared a Huguenot uprising after the attack on Coligny. The king may have shared this fear, and the idea of launching a pre-emptive strike may therefore have appealed to him [57 *p. 95*].

Be that as it may, Charles and his advisers certainly decided to wipe out the Huguenot leadership. Prime responsibility for this task was entrusted to the king's Swiss and French guards and to those of the duke of Anjou serving under the dukes of Guise and Aumale and other Catholic captains. The part played by the municipal authorities is less clear. Jean Le Charron, the Mayor of Paris, was called to the Louvre on 23 August. He was ordered by the king to take all necessary steps to secure the capital: he was to keep the gates shut, immobilise boats on the Seine, distribute arms to the militia and assemble artillery outside the Hôtel de Ville. He may also have received secret instructions, though we cannot assume that these ordered the general massacre that ensued.

The massacre allegedly started before daybreak on 24 August, when members of the king's guard, led by Guise and other Catholic nobles, broke into the Hôtel de Béthisy and murdered Coligny, tossing his body out of a window. Guise is said to have kicked it, and the head was then cut off and sent to the pope. A Catholic mob mutilated the headless corpse and dragged it through the streets for three days, before it was hanged at the gibbet of Montfaucon. The Admiral's remains were eventually cut down and secretly buried by his followers. His cruel end ensured him a place in the Pantheon of Protestant martyrs.

The tocsin of St Germain l'Auxerrois allegedly rang as the Admiral was being murdered and it is possible that words spoken by Guise as he left the Hôtel de Béthisy encouraged Parisian Catholics to rise against their Huguenot neighbours. Many were all too willing to believe that Charles IX had at last thrown his authority on the side of God's purpose of national purification [57 *p. 99*]. At 11 a.m. Le Charron called on the king, to complain of the bloodshed and slaughter sweeping through the capital. This hardly suggests that he had been ordered to unleash the massacre. That afternoon, in response to a royal command, he called a halt to the 'pillaging, sacking of houses and murders', but the slaughter continued for nearly a week. From the district of St Germain it spread south and east. Protestant sources contain horrific accounts of the atrocities committed. Such violent acts were often drawn from a store of punitive and purificatory traditions current in sixteenth-century France [53 *pp. 152–87*]. Thus the burning of a bookbinder mimicked the execution traditional for heresy. Likewise, the mutilation of Coligny's body was a ritual of humiliation as well as a parodying of royal justice. Among the first non-noble victims of the massacre were wealthy Huguenot merchants. Greed and jealousy often helped to fuel the violence, as did alcohol. Many of the murderers and looters were drunk. The violence, however, was not simply vindictive: Huguenots were forced to recite Catholic prayers or to go to Mass. Sometimes, too, there was extortion: at least one Huguenot saved his life by promising to pay a ransom of a thousand *écus*.

What role did the Parisian militia play in the massacre? According to one historian, Bourgeon, the king had lost control of the capital to the bourgeois militia, consisting of 5,000 armed men, led by 150 captains. Each captain was responsible for mobilising a *dizaine*, which was little more than a street and its immediate neighbourhood. Being in close touch with the inhabitants, such captains were well placed to harness opposition to the Crown's fiscal and religious policies. But whom did they obey? Bourgeon points to various possible leaders, including the former mayor, Claude Marcel, but he thinks it possible that they took their cue ultimately from Guise [35]. Diefendorf argues that the militia was less cohesive and shows that relatively few captains took part in the massacre. A close reading of even the Protestant sources suggests that the highest city officials kept aloof from the killing and may even have tried to restrain it. Not all Parisian Catholics became murderers. While some remained quietly in their homes, others offered protection to their Huguenot friends and neighbours. Yet many Catholics did approve of the slaughter. When an old hawthorn bush in the Cemetery of the Innocents suddenly sprang to life, they proclaimed it to be a miracle, indicating God's pleasure at the destruction of Coligny and his friends [57].

Was the massacre premeditated? Many contemporaries, both Catholics and Protestants, believed that it was. The Cardinal of Lorraine, for one, was anxious that his family of Guise should take the credit for it. Protestants, like Simon Goulart, were sure that the massacre had been planned as far back as 1570 and that the Edict of St Germain had been a clever ploy designed to lull Huguenots into a false sense of security. The idea that the massacre was premeditated is shared by some present-day historians. Bourgeon, for example, has suggested that Spain and probably the papacy were behind the plot to kill Coligny, and that the duke of Alba was a prime mover. 'Despite its unfolding', he writes, 'nothing, it seems, was less improvised than the St Bartholomew's day massacre' [35 *p. 62*]. The elimination of the Huguenot leadership, according to

Bourgeon, was meant to be the opening shot in a campaign orchestrated by Spain to force a complete change of royal policies in France: the annulment of the Navarre marriage, the abrogation of the Peace of St Germain, the return to power of the Guises, the exclusion of the Huguenots from the king's council, the *Parlement* and other bodies, a curb on taxation, the abandonment of French interference in the Low Countries and a realignment of French diplomacy in line with that of Spain and the pope. The truth, alas, will never be known. The only certainty is the decision taken by the king and his advisers on 23 August to wipe out the Huguenot leaders.

The massacre was not confined to Paris. It spread to a dozen or so French cities: Orléans, La Charité, Bourges, Saumur, Angers, Lyons, Troyes, Rouen, Bordeaux, Toulouse and Gaillac [139]. In most of these cities, the violence followed almost immediately on receipt of news of the Parisian massacre, while in a few it spread into the first week of October, almost a month and a half after the initial violence in the capital. In some cities, the killing was carried out by the authorities systematically and in cold blood; in others, it was instigated from below and the city was given over to looting and butchery on a scale that rivalled events in the capital.

Contemporary accounts of the provincial massacres suggest that those who did the killing believed that they were carrying out the king's wishes. Yet, in a series of letters, Charles IX expressly ordered his lieutenants to contain the violence. On 24 August he informed the provincial governors of the murders of Huguenot nobles at court, blaming them on the long-standing rivalry between the houses of Guise and Châtillon. He repeated his wish to see the Edict of St Germain strictly observed. On 27 and 28 August Charles sent out more letters. He urged his officers in the Midi to be vigilant lest the Huguenots should rise up to avenge the murders in Paris. To those in other parts, where Catholics were in the majority, he admitted his personal responsibility for the execution of the Huguenot leaders, justifying it as the necessary response to a plot which they had been hatching against himself. But he disclaimed responsibility for the mass violence afterwards, and urged the authorities everywhere to restore calm. Calvinists maintained that these letters from the king were merely a smokescreen aimed at concealing his true orders, which secret messengers had delivered by word of mouth. But the evidence does not support this. It seems that magistrates did try conscientiously to carry out the king's orders of 24–28 August. However, soon after the massacre began,

Charles IX sent verbal orders to a few provincial governors, calling for sterner measures against the Huguenots in their areas. These orders were quickly countermanded, but the king's hesitation played into the hands of Catholic extremists, who were looking for any pretext to wipe out their religious opponents. Soon after the massacre began in Paris, some influential Catholic nobles set out for the provinces or sent messengers to the areas under their authority, informing them that the king had ordered the extermination of the Huguenots throughout France. Confusion was sometimes compounded by false royal commands fabricated by extreme Catholics within the ruling élite of a particular town. But the receipt of letters from the court did not always produce a massacre.

Why were the Huguenots so unpopular in France in the 1570s? Their day-to-day behaviour, it seems, invited hostility. They set themselves apart from the rest of society by their sober clothes and high moral conduct, and they shocked Catholic sensibilities by abstaining from popular festivities, religious processions or the banquets of confraternities. The Huguenots also disrupted Catholic services and desecrated the host and religious images. Such attacks were seen by Catholics as a threat to the entire community, for this was an age that did not distinguish between the moral order and the natural world: an attack on a church or shrine seemed bound to arouse God's wrath, which might be expressed as a plague or flood. Catholic preachers often blamed the Huguenot minority within a community for some natural disaster. The only remedy, they argued, was for the minority to be removed. Hostility to the Huguenots was also in some cases a reaction to their risings in the first two civil wars, which had been followed by attacks on churches and by measures that discriminated against Catholics. In most French towns there was no violence in the wake of the massacre of St Bartholomew. Huguenots were often imprisoned for a short time for their own protection. The local authorities, moved by loyalty to the king and sometimes by fear that violence against the Huguenots might turn into an attack on the rich, generally managed to restrain the Catholics and protect the Huguenots from harm.

7 HUGUENOT SURVIVAL AND RESISTANCE

The Parisian Huguenots, it seems, offered little resistance to the massacre of St. Bartholomew's day. Most of them were dragged from their beds and killed before they could gather in self-defence. Their attitude also owed much to their faith: they accepted suffering as a trial imposed on them by God. However, there were also many who were persuaded to abjure their faith by the sheer magnitude of the massacre. They could not believe that God would have allowed such a slaughter of His own children. At the French court expectation was high that the Protestants would soon return to the Catholic church. Charles IX offered the Huguenot princes of Navarre and Condé one of three choices: conversion, death or life imprisonment. After a brief show of defiance by Condé, the two princes abjured. They were not the only ones to lapse. A contemporary reported that 5,000 Parisian Huguenots abjured after the massacre. Two years later, Jean de L'Espine stated that the French Protestant churches had lost more than two-thirds of their members. This is borne out by evidence from Rouen, where Catholic parish registers reveal a flood of rebaptisms of Calvinist children [30]. Many adult Huguenots submitted to a formal ceremony of abjuration in the cathedral. Altogether some 3,000 Huguenots in Rouen became Catholics. Others chose to emigrate, England being their preferred destination. Some went to Zeeland, while a handful risked the hazardous overland journey to Geneva. When Rouen's reformed church rose from the ashes after the pacification of 1573 it was but a shadow if its former self; it never regained its original strength.

THE UNITED PROVINCES OF THE MIDI

The impact of the massacre of St Bartholomew on the Huguenots in the south and centre-west of France was as profound as elsewhere, though after the initial panic it was inevitably softened by their numerical strength in those areas [65]. Although many Huguenot nobles had been killed in Paris, and Navarre and Condé were prisoners, there remained enough of the lesser nobility to work out a new defensive strategy, both military and political. Important towns controlled by the Huguenots, like La Rochelle, Montauban, Millau and Castres, closed their gates to royal agents, and in the Cévennes various fortresses turned themselves into independent islands. While the armies of Charles IX tried to reconquer Sancerre and La Rochelle, the Huguenots seized several fortified towns in Languedoc. The Governor of Languedoc, Henri de Montmorency-Damville, was ordered by the king to pacify the area.

Political activity was also intense. The Huguenot leaders made contact with each other, particularly in the Midi, and swore a solemn oath of union. More or less spontaneous assemblies of Huguenots met late in 1572 or 1573 at Réalmont, Millau, Montauban, Castres, Uzès and Nîmes. Although most of the people who attended these gatherings were Protestants, there were also some Catholics, who had been appalled by the massacre of St Bartholomew. The rules laid down by these assemblies determined the constitution of an independent state, which one historian has called 'the United Provinces of the Midi' [*Doc. 7*]. Especially important were the assemblies at Montauban (August 1573) and Millau (December 1573), for they envisaged a federal republic [65 *pp. 185–8*]. Supreme authority was vested in the Estates-General, an occasional body made up of representatives from each province having taken an oath of allegiance to the Protestant Union. The executive authority was a Protector, who had charge of military affairs and was assisted by a permanent council. Each province was allowed a considerable measure of autonomy within the federation: it was administered by a chamber, meeting periodically, a permanent executive council and a military commander for the region. A similar degree of independence was accorded to the towns and villages: the municipal authorities were empowered to administer local affairs, enforce law and order and control taxation. Justice was left in the main to magistrates of the *bailliages* and *présidiaux*, who were for the most part early converts to Protestantism. Cases on appeal were judged by special courts – one for each of the five provinces in the Union – with an equal number of Protestant and Catholic judges. The Huguenot republic was funded out of taxes normally paid to the Crown, the salt tax, confiscated ecclesiastical revenues and extraordinary levies on Huguenot churches. These revenues were administered by a federal controller, federal receivers and provincial controllers; the great towns had their own controllers and receivers [130, *pp. 149–53*].

The new French 'state within the state' resembled in some respects the Dutch United Provinces: both were federal republics in which military authority was exercised by a high-ranking nobleman, who was controlled by a permanent executive, and by a federal assembly, meeting periodically, in which the provinces of the union were all represented. But there was also much that was traditional in this Huguenot state, for the towns and villages of southern France had a long tradition of self-government. The provincial assemblies of the Huguenots were also comparable to the old provincial estates and *états particuliers**. It is likely that, except for an increase in taxation, local people did not see any great change between the new régime and the old, especially since the personnel remained essentially unchanged. Even so, the new state was revolutionary, since the federal assembly or Estates-General appointed the Protector, who exercised powers (*viz.*, the fixing and distribution of taxes, the appointment of ambassadors and generals, the making of laws) which hitherto had belonged exclusively to the king of France.

The effectiveness of the new state was limited by geographical factors and internal divisions. Only the Huguenots living south of a line drawn roughly from Grenoble in the east to St Jean d'Angély in the west were part of it; those living further north were excluded, even if they did sometimes send representatives to the southern assemblies. What is more, within the Huguenot state itself there were many large cities (Toulouse, Bordeaux, Marseilles, Avignon, Aix and Agen) which lay outside its control. Provence, the Toulouse region and many small areas near the Pyrenees remained Catholic. Constant friction also disturbed the relations between the great nobles who led the military operations, and members of the assemblies and councils. The Protectors were: first, the Prince of Condé, then Henri de Montmorency-Damville (who was a Catholic ally of the Union from 1574 to about 1579), and finally Henry of Navarre (who escaped from the French court in February 1576). These strong men did not take kindly to being controlled by an assembly dominated by Calvinist pastors and men of the robe (high magistrates of bourgeois origin). They were even less submissive to a permanent council whose *raison d'être* was to control their actions. When Navarre became heir-presumptive to the throne (1584) relations became even more strained. The Assembly of La Rochelle (1588) had to amend the membership and powers of the permanent council. Henceforth it was to consist of ten members, who would meet three times a week at Navarre's residence and discuss with him all the Union's affairs.

THE HUGUENOT DOCTRINE OF RESISTANCE

Politics and religion in the sixteenth century were generally regarded as inseparable. The ruler was seen as God's anointed, as His lieutenant on earth, and his subjects were supposed to follow his lead in matters of faith. Religious unity was generally regarded as essential to political unity, so that religious dissent or heresy was commonly identified with sedition. Thus if some of the king's subjects decided to depart from his religious faith, they opened themselves to the charge of political disobedience. This was why the great Protestant reformers, Luther, Calvin and Zwingli, although they were primarily concerned with religious issues, could not avoid considering the question of obedience to the secular ruler. If he chose to become a Protestant, the question did not arise, but if he preferred to remain a Catholic, then what political stance should his Protestant subjects take? The question became all the more critical if the ruler tried to maintain religious unity by forbidding religious dissent and persecuting those who disobeyed.

Luther addressed the question of political obedience in several writings [124, II *pp. 191–206*]. He took his cue from the text in St Paul's Epistle to the Romans: 'the powers that be are ordained of God'. But he did not include the Church among those powers, for his doctrine of justification by faith alone removed the need for a church with jurisdictional authority, standing as an intermediary between God and man. The Church, in Luther's view, was the invisible congregation of the people of God living from His word. This left the secular ruler as the only divinely ordained coercive force on earth. His duty, according to Luther, was to foster the preaching of the Gospel and to uphold the true faith. In other words, his power was not absolute: if he exceeded the limits of his authority by acting in an ungodly way, obedience was not due to him. The subject's duty was to follow his own conscience, as indicated by the Acts of the Apostles: 'we must obey God (who desires right) rather than man'. Yet Luther was no less insistent that the ruler must never be resisted. In his *Admonition to Peace* he reminded the German peasants that 'the fact that the rulers are wicked and unjust does not excuse disorder and rebellion'. In a later pamphlet Luther instructed the people that they should 'suffer everything that can happen rather than fight' against their lord and tyrant. But why should a tyrant be ordained of God? The answer, according to Luther, lay in man's sinfulness: the tyrant rules 'not because he is a scoundrel but because of people's sin'. Tyranny is a divine punishment for sin.

However, the attitude of Luther and his followers changed radically after 1530, when the Emperor Charles V tried to outlaw Protestantism. They were persuaded to endorse an idea derived from canon law justifying the use of force in self-defence. Thus Osiander argued that the powers-that-be referred to by St Paul included not merely the ruler but the 'inferior magistrates' as well. If the ruler failed to perform his duties, he could be lawfully resisted by the 'inferior magistrates'. The most important statement of the constitutional theory adopted by the Lutherans was the *Confession* of the pastors of Magdeburg (April 1550). This boldly asserted that 'whenever a superior magistrate persecutes his subjects, then, by the law of nature, by divine law and by the true religion and worship of God, the inferior magistrate ought by God's mandate to resist him'.

Until the last years of his life Calvin firmly adhered to the doctrine of non-resistance [124, II *pp. 191–4, 214*]. It was the subject's sacred duty, he declared, to obey the magistrate even if he was 'a very wicked man utterly unworthy of all honour'. For those who ruled unjustly and incompetently had been raised up by God 'to punish the wickedness of the people'. But there are signs that in the late 1550s Calvin began to move towards an acceptance of a constitutional theory of resistance. Writing to Coligny on 16 April 1561, he referred to a remark he had made before the Conspiracy of Amboise. He had strongly condemned resistance, but with an important reservation: 'I admitted, it is true, that if the princes of the blood demanded to be maintained in their rights for the common good, and if the courts of the *parlement* joined them in their quarrel, then it would be lawful for all good subjects to lend them armed resistance.' In his *Homilies on the First Book of Samuel*, Calvin endorsed the opinion that if the supreme magistrate failed in his office, the inferior magistrates had the right 'to constrain the prince in his office and even to coerce him' in the name of upholding good and godly government. Yet even in the 1560s Calvin continued to insist that the exceptions he had begun to allow did not include the possibility of resistance by individual citizens or the body of the people.

During the French Wars of Religion the political ideas of the Huguenots became extremely radical as a direct consequence of their political experiences. But at first Calvin's followers tried to avoid any direct confrontation with the government of Catherine de' Medici, pinning their hopes on achieving a measure of religious toleration. They could feel reasonably optimistic about Catherine's policy. As she quickly perceived, her best hope of retaining power in the 1560s was to give the Huguenots some religious liberty. At the Colloquy of Poissy she allowed their spokesman, Théodore de Bèze, to be heard on the same terms as his Catholic adversaries [*Doc. 3*]. After the colloquy had failed, she tried to avert a conflict by promulgating the Edict of January 1562 in which she guaranteed the Huguenots freedom of worship everywhere except in the cities. Even as late as August 1570, they were allowed a significant measure of religious freedom in the Edict of St Germain.

The idea of religious toleration as something virtuous in itself was not unknown in sixteenth-century France. In 1544, for example, Guillaume Postel argued in his *The Concord of the World* against the need to enforce religious uniformity [124, II *pp. 244–5*]. The truths of Christianity were so obvious, in his opinion, that they were bound to commend themselves sooner or later to all reasonable men. Another advocate of religious toleration was Sebastian Castellio. All religious persecution, in his view, was based on a presumption of certainty about questions over which certainty can never be attained: thus the forcing of individual consciences is never justified. A similar view was expressed by the great philosopher Jean Bodin. In his *Six Books of the Commonwealth* he condemns those who try to force others to accept their own religious opinions [124, II *pp. 248–9*]. Writers such as Postel, Castellio and Bodin believed that religious persecution was morally indefensible, but it was also possible to regard it as tactically mistaken. This view was probably more widespread among sixteenth-century Frenchmen than the moral one. While they valued religious uniformity, they did not feel that it was worth preserving at the cost of destroying the commonwealth. This was the characteristic view of the so-called *politique* party, and it was most eloquently expressed by the French Chancellor, Michel de l'Hôpital, in a series of speeches to the Estates-General [*Doc. 2*] In his judgement religious uniformity was not essential to the well-being of France, and the only sane policy for the French government was to give up religious unity for the sake of domestic peace. The *Exhortation to the Princes*, a tract of 1561 that has been attributed to Etienne Pasquier, argued likewise. The only solution to France's current crisis, it claimed, was to permit two churches within the state, 'one Roman and the other Protestant' [124, II *pp. 251–2*].

Sensible as these views were, they failed to carry the day, as we have seen. The massacre of Vassy in March 1562 provoked an armed rising of Huguenots under the Prince of Condé. In a *Declaration* he justified his resort to arms by accusing the Guises of usurping the lawful government. His purpose, he declared, was 'to uphold the observation of the edicts and ordinances of the king's majesty'. But, as the violence continued and Catherine de' Medici gave up her efforts at conciliation, it became increasingly difficult for the Huguenots to maintain that they were simply defending the lawful government against the Guises. After failing to capture the king and blockade Paris, Condé issued another manifesto in which he accused the government of perverting the French constitution. Similar arguments were used in a large number of anonymous pamphlets published in 1567 and 1568. But it was the massacre of St Bartholomew (1572) and the role played by King Charles IX and his mother in that tragic event which made it impossible for the Huguenots to justify their armed insurrection in terms of defending the Crown. How could they profess loyalty to a monarchy that had connived at so foul a deed? How could they distinguish between the king and his 'evil counsellors' when it was clear to everyone that they were equally guilty?

As the Huguenot cities, following the lead of La Rochelle, repudiated their loyalty to the Crown, it became necessary to find a new justification for their armed resistance. All the Huguenot writers accepted the thesis that ever since the massacre of Vassy the Catholics, inspired mainly by the Cardinal of Lorraine, had conspired to exterminate the Protestants. Catherine de' Medici, it was alleged, had been a party to the plot, at least since her meeting with the duke of Alba at Bayonne in 1565. Underlying the Huguenot pamphlets of the 1570s was a myth strongly tinged with xenophobia. The recent massacre was interpreted as a manifestation of the queen-mother's Italianism. 'Among all nations', wrote Henri Estienne, 'Italy carries off the prize for cunning and subtlety, so it is in Italy with Tuscany, and in Tuscany with Florence.' Catherine was seen as the disciple of that quintessential Florentine, Machiavelli, whose spectre had begun to haunt Protestant Europe. Stories were told that Catherine had brought up her children on Machiavelli's *Prince*, that her son, Henry of Anjou, carried it in his pocket, and that the massacre was the direct application of its advice to commit all necessary cruelties in a single blow. In 1576 Innocent Gentillet, a Huguenot who fled to Geneva after the massacre, published his *Anti-Machiavel*, a long and furious tirade which helped to create the legend of Machiavelli as the satanic author of text-books for tyrants. He blamed Machiavelli directly for the 'infamous vices' which were taking root in the French government, and thereby helped the Huguenots to present their resistance as a necessary and legitimate act of self-defence [124, II *pp. 308–9]*.

Among the great volume of Huguenot political theory to appear after 1572, three works call for special notice on account of their originality and importance: the *Francogallia* by François Hotman (1573) [7; 10]; the *Right of Magistrates* by Théodore de Bèze (1574) [6; 7] and the *Vindiciae contra tyrannos* (1579) [4; 7]. On the surface the *Francogallia* is a work of antiquarianism: it deals with Gauls, Romans and Franks, and carefully eschews contemporary historians and events [7 *pp. 48–50; 85 pp. 238–60]*. But the dedication clearly indicates its relevance to the contemporary situation. Hotman deplores the fact that for twelve years his country has been scorched by the fires of civil wars; he assumes that France's ancient constitution carries legal validity for his own day and stresses (in accordance with a view expressed by Claude de Seyssel in the early sixteenth century) that the Crown must always be controlled by the three checks of *police**, religion and justice. All France's current problems, Hotman argues, are the consequence of an attack by King Louis XI on her ancient constitution: the Crown has usurped the functions that had originally been exercised by the three estates [*Doc. 8*]. According to Hotman, the king was originally elected by the people's representatives, who retained the power of control over his actions. The king, in brief, was really only a 'magistrate of the whole people'; they could make him and unmake him. Here was a historically based theory of popular sovereignty which could be used by the Huguenots to discredit the Valois government and to gain wider support for their revolution (124, II *pp. 310–16]*.

De Bèze wrote the *Right of Magistrates* in 1573, following a period of intense political activity. Like Hotman, with whom he was in touch, de Bèze believed that resistance to a lawful government could only pertain to officers and institutions endowed with part of that government's authority. But whereas Hotman had vested the right of resistance in the Estates-General, de Bèze shared it between the Estates and the inferior magistrates [*Doc. 9*]. For he knew that the Estates-General met infrequently and were not always free. De Bèze had two sorts of 'inferior magistrates' in mind: high-ranking nobles holding hereditary offices in national or provincial government, and the elected magistrates who administered many French cities [6 *pp. vii–xlvii; 124, II pp. 315–16]*.

The authorship of the *Vindiciae contra tyrannos* has been disputed, but the likeliest author is Philippe Du Plessis-Mornay, who in 1579 was a young nobleman actively engaged in the religious wars in France. This may explain why his treatise was particularly well adapted to the immediate needs of the Huguenot movement [7, *pp. 138–40*; 124, II *pp. 325–7*]. Mornay knew that, as a minority, the Huguenots could not look to the Estates-General as a means of achieving their ends. He preferred to vest the right of resistance in the 'inferior magistrates'. Mornay examines at length the nature of the state and its origins. These he sees as the result of two contracts: the first, between God and the king, by which the latter promises that his commands 'are not in conflict with God's laws'; and the second, between God and the people, to ensure that the king's duties are correctly fulfilled [*Doc. 12*]. It follows from this twofold contractual system that if the king fails to do his duty to uphold the Church and the law of God, the 'inferior magistrates' must not only resist him, but also remove him. If they fail to do so, they will 'very gravely sin against the covenant with God'.

Many historians have been inclined to think that the Huguenot doctrine of resistance was an essentially Calvinistic creation. In fact, the arguments used by the first Calvinist revolutionaries in the 1550s were of largely Lutheran inspiration, while the new arguments added in the 1570s looked back to the medieval schoolmen [124, II *pp. 210, 320*]. They owed much to the radical elements in civil and canon law, and also to the whole tradition of conciliarist thought stemming from d'Ailly and Gerson at the start of the fifteenth century. By appealing to natural-law arguments the Huguenot writers were able to base their theory of popular sovereignty on the logical, and not merely chronological, origins of the state. This in turn allowed them to present their case for resistance as a purely political, non-sectarian argument capable of appealing not merely to Protestants but even to Catholic moderates and malcontents. Indeed, one of the ironies of the age was the way in which the revolutionary arguments of the Huguenots were taken over in the 1580s by their religious opponents. Following the death of the duke of Anjou in June 1584, the Huguenot leader, Henry of Navarre, became heir-presumptive to the throne. Consequently, the Huguenots rallied to support the hereditary principle and the Salic law*, while the Catholic League sought to justify its efforts to keep Henry off the throne. The doctrine of the *Vindiciae* suddenly became an acute embarrassment to the Huguenots and useful to the Catholics.

8 THE CATHOLIC LEAGUE

While the massacre of St Bartholomew wiped out many Protestant nobles, it did not destroy the will to survive among their co-religionists of inferior social standing. A few weeks after the massacre, the Protestants of La Rochelle refused to admit the governor, Marshal Biron. Charles IX accordingly declared war on the city and appointed his brother Henry, duke of Anjou, to lead his army. Thus began the fourth religious war. In May 1573, however, Anjou was elected king of Poland and obliged to accept the religious toleration existing in that country [45 pp. 181–231]. Meanwhile, all his efforts to take La Rochelle by storm had failed. On 6 July, therefore, he lifted the siege and soon afterwards left for Poland. The peace that followed fell far short of what the Huguenots had wanted: they were permitted to practise their faith in private and in three cities (La Rochelle, Montauban and Nîmes); elsewhere they were granted only freedom of conscience. Such a settlement could not last; it led to 'a fluctuating state of increasingly dangerous chaos which favored all ambitious malcontents and fishers in troubled waters' [127 p. 213].

   Chief among the malcontents was Francis, duke of Alençon, youngest son of Catherine de' Medici. A sickly youth of limited ability, he was deeply jealous of his elder brother, Anjou, and hoped to succeed him as Lieutenant-General of the kingdom. When this hope was frustrated, he engaged in a series of plots, all of them unsuccessful. Alençon is often seen as the leader of a party of *politiques**, that is to say, moderate Catholics and Protestants who favoured religious toleration. But the group of unprincipled adventurers who helped him pursue his private ambitions hardly deserves to be called a 'party' [78 p. 38]. A more serious trouble-maker was Henri de Montmorency-Damville, son of the old Constable of Montmorency, and Governor of Languedoc, who, in asserting his own quasi-independent authority in the south, did advocate a policy of religious compromise.

On 30 May 1574 Charles IX died and Catherine de' Medici declared herself regent pending the return of Anjou – now Henry III – from Poland. He was expected home soon, but he spent so much time being entertained in Germany and Italy that it was not till September that he reached Lyons. One of his first tasks was to impose his authority on Damville, who, early in 1575, moved into open revolt after making an alliance with the southern Huguenots [45 *pp. 270–4*]. But Henry seemed more concerned to reorganise his council and the etiquette of his court than to lead a military campaign. Abandoning the south, he went to Rheims for his coronation (13 February 1575) and his marriage to Louise de Vaudémont, a member of the house of Lorraine.

Modern opinion is divided about Henry III. Past historians, it is claimed, have been brainwashed by the torrent of contemporary hostile propaganda [34; 40; 45]. He was an intelligent ruler who sponsored much reforming legislation (even if it was not always enforced) and showed a lively interest in intellectual matters. Yet Henry invited criticism by his public behaviour. Apart from indulging in foppish ways of his own, he surrounded himself with young male favourites (who became known as *mignons**) and condoned, if he did not actually encourage, their scandalous conduct, which often spilled on to the streets of Paris [*Doc. 11*] [34 *pp. 23–6*]. The extravagance of the court, reflected in its absurd fashions and lavish entertainments, seemed a poor excuse for the heavy taxes repeatedly imposed by the king on his subjects. French xenophobia was also fuelled by the amount of influence exerted at court by Italian merchants and bankers. Public opinion was shocked by the king's displays of Catholic piety, revealing an almost perverted pleasure in self-mortification. Another offence, mainly to aristocratic sensibility, was the excessive generosity shown by Henry to two of his *mignons*: Anne, duke of Joyeuse, and Jean-Louis de Nogaret, duke of Épernon. From 1586 onwards the latter controlled not only the privy purse but also access to the king [33 *pp. 23–7*].

In September 1575 Alençon managed to slip away from court, where he had been kept under surveillance, and at Dreux set about raising an army. His motives are unclear. He probably intended to join Damville and the Huguenots, but, being penniless, he soon made a truce with his mother, who had been sent to defuse the situation. However, she could not prevent an invasion of eastern France by an army of German mercenaries recently raised as a result of talks between Condé and John Casimir, son of the Elector Palatine. To complicate the situation further, Henry of Navarre escaped from the French court in February 1576 and promptly reverted to the Protestant faith which he had been forced to abjure in 1572 [22 *p. 211*]. Soon afterwards a delegation representing Alençon, Navarre, Condé and Damville presented Henry III with a long catalogue of grievances.

Finding himself powerless in the face of a huge Protestant force, Henry ended the war. On 5 May 1576 he issued the Edict of Beaulieu, which has come to be known as the Peace of Monsieur, because of the contemporary assumption that it had been forced on the king by Alençon (who, as the king's younger brother, was referred to as 'Monsieur') [*Doc. 10*]. For the first time in the religious wars the Huguenots were allowed the 'free, public and general exercise' of their religion. They were permitted to own and build churches, to hold consistories and synods, and to occupy eight surety towns (*places de sûreté**). An important clause provided for the creation of special tribunals (*chambres mi-parties**) in the *parlements*, comprising an equal number of Catholic and Protestant judges. The edict was accompanied by various concessions to nobles who had opposed the Crown: thus Damville was reinstated as Governor of Languedoc, though in practice he had never relinquished the office; and Alençon, who now became duke of Anjou, received three duchies and a large pension (19 *pp. 97–120*; 127 *pp. 361–2*].

The peace caused widespread indignation among Catholics, who viewed it as a royal capitulation to the Huguenot party. Some of them decided to oppose its implementation and to set up new defensive leagues. On hearing that Condé had been made Governor of Picardy, Jacques d'Humières, Governor of Péronne, begged the king not to hand over his city to a Protestant garrison. One hundred and fifty nobles of the province, led by two clients of the Guises, gathered round him. Secret meetings were held in support of their action, bringing together representatives of the three estates. Under an elected council this league set itself the aim of defending the Catholic faith. Other towns of Picardy joined the movement and comparable associations arose elsewhere, notably in Poitou and Brittany. The king suspected the duke of Guise, his brother Mayenne and the duke of Nemours of being at the head of the movement, and in August he made them swear an oath to observe the Peace of Monsieur. In fact, Guise responsibility for the league in Picardy has never been proved [49 *pp. 81–2*].

The mounting defiance on the part of the Catholic League forced Henry III to act. Instead of resisting it directly, he tried to take over the movement's leadership. The success of the policy was put to the test at the Estates-General of Blois in December 1576. Only one Huguenot attended the meeting, while the League was heavily represented in all three estates. Henry tried to focus the deputies' attention on domestic reform, but they called for the destruction of the Huguenots. The king replied that he was willing to reopen hostilities with them if he was given the means, but the third estate refused to vote for the necessary taxes. This left Henry committed to a new war but without the means to fight it. Before the war was resumed, however, Catherine de' Medici managed to detach Damville from his alliance with the Huguenots, and Anjou accepted a royal command against them. In the fighting that ensued, he captured La Charité and sacked Issoire [78 *p. 90*]. But, lacking the means to follow up his advantage, Henry III had to sign the Peace of Bergerac (25 September 1577). The Edict of Poitiers, which confirmed the peace, was very similar in form and substance to that of May 1576. A major difference, however, was the restriction of Huguenot worship in public to the towns already held by the Protestants and to one place per *bailliage*. The edict also banned all leagues and associations throughout the kingdom [19 *pp. 131–53*; 127 *pp. 362–3*].

When Anjou returned to court in January 1578 he soon became involved in intrigues and scandals. On 10 January 300 of his followers, led by Bussy d'Amboise, challenged Henry III's *mignons* 'to fight it out to the death', and, on 27 April, a duel took place between the king's *mignons* and some friends of Guise. Two were killed on each side, and Henry showed his grief by giving the dead *mignons* a superb marble tomb. According to L'Estoile, the king's conduct on this occasion further damaged his reputation among the Parisians, while boosting that of the Guises [12 *p. 187*]. Soon afterwards, Guise left the court; meanwhile Anjou went to Angers to raise an army for service in the Low Countries. In July, he occupied Mons and, in August, reached an agreement with the Dutch estates: in return for military support, he was given the title of 'Defender of the liberty of the Netherlands against the tyranny of the Spaniards and their allies'. But Anjou's ambition led him astray almost at once, for the Netherlands were as much opposed to a French invasion as to a Spanish one. In the autumn the duke reopened his marriage negotiations with Elizabeth of England [78 *pp. 101–7*].

In October 1578 Catherine de' Medici travelled south on another peace mission. She signed a treaty with the Huguenots at Nérac (February 1579), had talks with Damville, and presided over a meeting of the estates of Languedoc. Wherever she went she urged mutual understanding, while stressing the need to obey the king above all. The queen-mother also managed to pacify a local conflict in Provence, but the situation in the south remained precarious, and the presence at the court at Nérac of Navarre's frivolous wife, Marguerite de Valois, did not make for stability. Her amorous intrigues, which rivalled those of her husband, prompted her brother, Henry III, to make fun of the court of Navarre. This gave the Huguenots of the south a good pretext for taking up arms again. However, it was in northern France that the so-called Lovers' War – the seventh of the Wars of Religion – began, when Henri de Condé seized the border town of La Fère (November 1579). Hostilities soon flared up in the south and, in May, Navarre first made his mark as a military leader by storming Cahors [22 *pp. 273–8*; 38 *p. 11*]. The Protestants of the Midi, however, were divided about the war, most of them preferring to keep the peace. Anjou was also opposed to the war, which threatened to upset his plans in the Netherlands. In November 1580 he negotiated the Peace of Fleix. This confirmed the treaties of Bergerac and Nérac and allowed the Huguenots to keep their surety towns for another six years, except Cahors which they had to give back.

Having settled the latest civil war, Anjou hoped that Henry III would back his enterprise in the Netherlands by giving him adequate funds. But Henry and his mother were most anxious to avoid being dragged into a war with Spain, so Anjou received only minimal support from his brother. In August he seized Cambrai, but soon fell back to the Channel coast. He visited England in October and made a pact with Elizabeth, but it soon became obvious that she had no intention of marrying him. On returning to the Netherlands, Anjou took the title of duke of Brabant. By October 1582, however, he was desperate. 'Everything is falling apart in ruin', he wrote, 'and the worst part of it is that I was given hopes which had led me too far to back down now...'. An attempt by him to seize Antwerp (January 1583) ended disastrously. The following October he returned to France for good. Even if he had been properly financed, his personal failings would probably have led to the same result [78 *pp. 195–200*].

On 10 June 1584 Anjou died of tuberculosis and with him died the hope which many Frenchmen had placed on his succession to the throne. His loss also raised a great threat to the Catholic cause, for Henry III had no son and seemed unlikely ever to have one. This left the Huguenot leader, Henry of Navarre, as heir presumptive to the throne under the Salic law. He was invited by Henry III to come to court and abjure his faith, but he refused. This situation led to the creation of a new league for the defence of the Catholic faith. In September 1584 Henry, duke of Guise, his brothers, the duke of Mayenne and the Cardinal of Guise, and two other noblemen met at Nancy and founded an association with the unambiguous aim of keeping Navarre off the throne [49 *pp. 128–9*]. They tried to gain the support of Pope Gregory XIII, but he was not keen to encourage a movement hostile to Henry III, whose Catholicism could not be faulted. Philip II of Spain, on the other hand, could not easily forgive the support given by the house of Valois to the Dutch rebels. Consequently, he authorised his agents to sign the Treaty of Joinville with Guise (31 December 1584). Places were reserved in the alliance for the dukes of Nevers and Mercoeur. The Guises and Spain undertook to defend the Catholic faith and to extirpate Protestantism from France and the Netherlands. Ruling out the possibility of a heretic succeeding to the French throne, they recognised the Cardinal of Bourbon, Henry of Navarre's uncle, as rightful heir [137]. The decrees of the Council of Trent were to become 'fundamental laws' in France. The future king was to renounce France's alliance with the Turks and stop French privateering at Spain's expense. Philip II for his part promised to subsidise an armed rising by the League.

Military operations began at once. Guise seized Chalon, while Mayenne captured Dijon, Mâcon and Auxonne. As governors of Champagne and Burgundy respectively they rallied their supporters and tried to recruit new ones, while Mercoeur, Elbeuf and Aumale stirred up agitation in Brittany, Normandy and Picardy. Much of north and central France soon fell under Guise control, and the old Cardinal of Bourbon, the League's candidate for the throne, was taken to Rheims. Yet the military and financial assistance promised to Guise by his allies did not materialise at once, and he might have run into serious difficulties if Catherine de' Medici had not prevented Henry III from acting swiftly to restore his authority. Her attitude may have been caused by resentment of the Épernon régime. Be this as it may, her action enabled reinforcements to reach Guise in time. On 31 March 1585 he published the Manifesto of Péronne, setting out the reasons which had led 'the cardinal of Bourbon, the princes, peers and lords of the cities and communities' to oppose those who were seeking to subvert the Catholic religion and the state. The manifesto emphasised the threat of persecution facing Catholics in the event of a Protestant becoming king. It denounced the recent warlike acts of the Huguenots and urged Catholics to prepare for a renewal of civil war. Joyeuse and Épernon were attacked without being named for paving the way to the throne of a heretic. They were also accused of depriving some nobles of their titles and others of their powers in order to achieve complete control over the armed forces. The manifesto called for the abolition of all taxes and extraordinary subsidies introduced since the reign of Charles IX and for triennial meetings of the Estates-General [47 *pp. 499–500*].

Under threat of invasion by foreign mercenaries in the pay of the League, Henry III sent to Switzerland for troops and took steps to defend Paris against a surprise attack. At the same time he looked for a diplomatic solution of the crisis. But the Leaguers used the talks that began on 9 April to consolidate their military position. The main stumbling block to an agreement was the surety towns demanded by Guise and his supporters. The Leaguers suggested that the king should draw up an edict against heresy, which their own forces would put into effect. On 7 July the Treaty of Nemours was signed [127 *p. 364*]. It was profoundly humiliating to Henry III, who undertook to pay the troops which had been raised against him. He also conceded surety towns to the Leaguers. The king may have hoped to get round the new treaty as he had done after the Peace of Monsieur, but the situation now was quite different: Guise had the backing not only of the Catholic nobility, but also of a number of towns, including Paris.

There were many reasons for the popular support gathered by the League. The prospect of a Protestant succeeding to the throne struck genuine fear into the hearts of many town-dwellers. The League seemed to them the realisation of a Christian ideal whose triumph would safeguard their eternal salvation. It also offered them hope of a change of régime. The reforms that had been laid down in the Ordinance of Blois (1579) had so far been largely ineffective: justice was as badly administered as ever, war was endemic, pillaging by troops was rife, taxes were getting heavier all the time, the venality of offices continued to flourish. What is more, the price of bread had doubled between 1578 and 1586, causing much hardship among the urban masses. All of this, in addition to the personal unpopularity of Henry III and his favourites, assisted the cause of Guise and his allies.

Among the towns that supported the League, Paris was the most radical. It set up its own organisation, which became known as the Sixteen (*les seize*) after the number of districts in the capital from which members of the central committee were elected [25; 26; 55; 120 *pp. 235–66*; 152; 157; 185]. The Parisian League was set up late in 1584 by Charles Hotman, *sieur* de La Rocheblond, and three clerics: Jean Prévost, Jean Boucher and Mathieu de Launoy. They nominated other Catholic zealots and respectable Parisians to join them. The recruitment was carefully done, each new member being required to take an oath of secrecy and loyalty. Even so, a royal agent, Nicolas Poulain, managed to infiltrate the movement and kept the king informed of what was taking place. His testimony shows that from the beginning close relations existed between the Sixteen and the duke of Guise. While the Sixteen managed to penetrate all the major institutions in Paris, including the *Parlement*, the other 'sovereign courts', the Châtelet and the university, arms were transported at night to the Hôtel de Guise, the duke's residence in the capital. An elaborate propaganda campaign made up of hundreds of printed pamphlets warned that the Huguenots were planning a massacre of Catholics and Navarre's accession to the throne. At the same time an agent was sent to Chartres, Orléans, Blois, Tours and other towns with a request for financial help for the Catholic reconquest of the kingdom.

It soon became clear that Henry III had no intention of fighting the Huguenots with any vigour. Returning to his devotions, he left affairs of state to his mother. Only the League took the war seriously: while Mercoeur defeated Condé in Brittany and Anjou, Mayenne fought Turenne in Saintonge and Périgord. Soon the conflict degenerated into desultory provincial campaigns. During the winter of 1586 Navarre won time by lengthy negotiations with the queen-mother. Meanwhile, his agents were raising an army in Germany. It was intended to join Navarre after crossing the whole of France. In August 1587 Henry III unexpectedly announced that he would take the field at the head of his troops. His plan of campaign, had it succeeded, might have restored his authority in the kingdom. While he himself waited on the Loire with the bulk of the army, he sent Joyeuse with crack troops to fight Navarre in the south-west, and ordered Guise with inadequate forces to oppose the German invasion. His secret hope was that Guise would be defeated and that Joyeuse would throw back the Huguenots. But fate determined otherwise: on 20 October 1587 Joyeuse was defeated and killed at Coutras; soon afterwards Guise routed the Germans at Auneau [45 *pp. 602–6*]. These were the main engagements of the so-called 'War of the Three Henries' (Henry III, Henry of Guise and Henry of Navarre). Henry III returned to Paris shortly after Christmas 1587.

He attended a Te Deum at Notre-Dame and organised a splendid funeral ceremony for Joyeuse. But the plaudits of the Parisians could not conceal the fact that the only victorious commanders of the recent war had been the king's enemies: Guise and Navarre. Fearing that if Guise came to Paris he would be given a hero's reception, Henry III banished him to his *gouvernement* of Champagne.

Early in 1588 Guise and the other principal Leaguers met at Nancy and drew up a list of demands for presentation to the king [49 *p. 162*]. In particular they asked for the dismissal of Épernon, the acceptance of Guise tutelage in the war against heresy, and publication of the decrees of the Council of Trent. The pope, Sixtus V, was anxious to reconcile Guise with Henry III, but the duke did not want a settlement that would downgrade his own role. He wanted the governorship of Normandy as a reward for his victory over the Germans, but Henry appointed Épernon instead. This move, as Pasquier noted, lost the king more nobles than he had lost at the battle of Coutras. The conviction that Épernon was fast leading the monarchy to its doom caused the archbishop of Lyons to join the League.

The tension that had been building up for some time between the king and the duke of Guise exploded in Paris during May 1588 [49 *pp. 166–79*]. Henry had forbidden the duke to enter the capital, but Guise defied the ban in response to an invitation from the Sixteen. Accompanied by a handful of nobles, he began by visiting Catherine de' Medici, who, overcoming her dismay, took him in her own carriage to the Louvre. Guise tried to justify his conduct to the king, who chose not to arrest him. During the night of 11 May, however, Henry introduced Swiss and French troops into the capital and posted them at various strategic points. The king's plan was allegedly to round up Guise's supporters and have them executed as an example to the rest. But the Parisians did not take kindly to the king's violation of their traditional right of self-defence. Crowds of agitators poured into the streets and erected barricades. The king's troops found themselves surrounded and under attack from the mob, while ministers sent by Henry to assist them ran into serious trouble. At first Guise did nothing to appease the mob, but eventually he responded to an appeal from the king and rode through the streets. Such was his charisma that he was soon able to bring the royal troops to safety. But the people of Paris remained under arms and some planned to march on the Louvre. On 13 May, Henry III and his courtiers managed to slip away unnoticed. Thus ended the famous 'Day of the Barricades' [*Doc. 13*]. The League had won control of Paris, but the king, without whom its actions could not be validated, had slipped through its fingers.

On 14 May the Bastille surrendered and Guise appointed a new governor. Next day the Mayor of Paris was imprisoned and replaced by La Chapelle-Marteau, a leader of the Sixteen. He was assisted by four new *échevins** of similar political complexion. Despite their radical views they all belonged to the merchant community. By substituting a *procureur de la ville* for the *procureur du roi** they aimed to strengthen municipal autonomy, but the League met with resistance from many Parisians loyal to their former notables. Guise, in the meantime, occupied various towns around Paris so as to guarantee its supplies in preparation for an eventual confrontation with the king. This, however, did not happen, largely because of Catherine de' Medici's mediating activities. In the end, Henry III accepted nearly all the League's demands in a new Edict of Union: he dismissed Épernon, reaffirmed the Treaty of Nemours, recognised the Cardinal of Bourbon as heir-presumptive to the throne, bestowed new governorships on the Guises and appointed the duke as Lieutenant-General of the kingdom.

Henry III, however, was playing for time. On 8 September he surprised everyone by sacking all his chief ministers. He may have wanted to rid himself of men who had favoured Catherine's conciliatory policy. In their place he chose to rely on the *surintendant**, François d'O, the *contrôleur-général*, Chenailles, the keeper of the seals, Montholon, and two new secretaries of state, Ruzé and Revol. Henry also called the Estates-General in an attempt to isolate the upper nobility, especially the Guises [101, *pp. 309–15*]. He tried to influence the elections, but most of the deputies supported the League. The presidents of the three estates – Cardinals Bourbon and Guise for the clergy, the count of Brissac for the nobility and La Chapelle-Marteau for the third estate – were all prominent Leaguers. The difference between the king and most of the deputies concerned mainly taxation and the nature of royal authority. Henry III agreed conditionally to some of the deputies' fiscal demands, but the third estate, instead of being satisfied, tried to impose its will upon him. Monarchs, it claimed, owed their authority to the Estates. 'Why then', asked the deputies, 'should the decisions taken by ourselves in this assembly be controlled by the king's council?' Weak as Henry III had often shown himself in the past, he was not prepared to ignore such a challenge to his authority. He decided to silence the third estate by striking a fatal blow at its aristocratic sponsors. On 23 October Guise was lured to the king's chamber at Blois and brutally murdered by Henry's bodyguard. Next day the Cardinal of Guise was also murdered, while other prominent Leaguers and members of the Guise family were thrown into prison [49 *pp. 9–19*].

Henry III tried to justify his action by claiming that the Guises had planned his deposition and death, but no one believed him. The Estates soon wound up their business without expressing much disapproval of the king's action, but in France at large news of the murders caused an explosion of grief and anger. Nowhere was this felt more than in Paris, where preachers took to the streets crying out for vengeance on the 'new Herod'. On 7 January 1589 the Sorbonne released all Frenchmen from their oath of loyalty to the king and sent its decision to Rome for papal approval. The murder of a cardinal was, of course, a heinous crime in the eyes of the Church, and, in May, Sixtus V summoned Henry to Rome to explain his conduct under threat of excommunication. Meanwhile, a new administration was set up in Paris. Special committees in each quarter of the capital elected representatives to a council of the Union. In February they established a General Council of forty members, which appointed Charles, duke of Mayenne, the last surviving brother of Guise, as Lieutenant-General of the kingdom. He lacked the charm and charisma of the murdered duke, but he was politically astute and had built up a powerful clientèle in Burgundy [58]. The General Council quickly went into action: it sent instructions and exhortations to other towns and very soon all the major Catholic cities, except Lyons, declared for the League. Within Paris itself, the General Council purged the *Parlement* of royalist judges, replacing them with its own nominees. It raised revenues by means of voluntary contributions, fines and property confiscations, and it took measures to defend the capital.

On 5 January 1589 Catherine de' Medici died, leaving Henry III very isolated. He was caught as in a vice between the forces of the League to the north and east and those of the Huguenots to the south. The king had control of three towns on the Loire (Tours, Blois, Beaugency), of Bordeaux, and of the provinces of Berri and Dauphiné. He badly needed a powerful ally, but a reconciliation with Mayenne was unthinkable. The only alternative was Henry of Navarre, who was already throwing out peace feelers. On 26 April the two Henries signed a truce; four days later they met at Plessis-les-Tours and sealed their accord. Combining their armies, they marched on Paris, capturing Senlis and Pontoise on the way. As

they laid siege to the capital – Henry III at St-Cloud and Navarre at
Meudon – a frenzy of anti-Valois sentiment took hold of the
Parisians. Processions invoked the help of the Almighty; preachers
clamoured for the extermination of Henry III as the agent of Satan.
Among those who heard the message was a young Jacobin friar
called Jacques Clément. On 1 August he made his way from Paris to
the king's camp. Claiming that he carried a message from some of
the king's friends in the capital, he was admitted to the royal
presence. As Henry invited him to come closer, Clément stabbed
him in the abdomen [*Doc. 15*]. A few hours later Henry died. One
of his last acts was to recognise Navarre as his heir, and to warn
him that he would only gain the throne by becoming a Catholic.

THE POLITICAL THOUGHT OF THE CATHOLIC LEAGUE

Few Catholics before 1560 challenged the king's right to full
obedience and complete sovereignty. Those who did were mostly
lawyers, who looked to the past for constitutional checks on the
monarch for purely secular reasons. Catholic support for the
monarchy became even stronger in the 1560s, as the Huguenots
sought to justify their armed resistance. They were accused of
seeking to abolish the monarchy in favour of a republic on the Swiss
model. Such works as *The Right of Magistrates* and the *Vindiciae*
were denounced by the Catholics as incitements to popular
rebellion. But the mood of Catholics changed dramatically in 1576,
following the Peace of Monsieur, which many regarded as much too
generous to the Huguenots. They began to cast doubt on Henry III's
interest in rooting out heresy. The manifesto of the League set up in
1576 contained a number of clauses going beyond its stated aim of
defending the Catholic church. One called for 'the restoration to the
provinces and their estates of their ancient rights, pre-eminences,
freedoms, and liberties such as they were in the time of King
Clovis'. While swearing obedience to Henry III and his successors,
the Leaguers agreed to resist, by force if necessary, *anyone* who
refused to accept their stated principles. When the Estates-General
met at Blois in 1576 an attempt was made to turn the Catholicism
of the monarchy into a 'fundamental law' of the French kingdom,
and this led to a protracted discussion of the 'fundamental laws' in
Catholic writings of the next twenty years [27 *p. 57*]. No one
doubted their existence (almost everyone agreed that they were a
body of custom by which France had been governed since
Pharamond, the legendary king of the Franks), but there was

argument over their number and scope. The lack of precise definition enabled the League to argue that it was a 'fundamental law' that the king of France should always be a Catholic. When the Protestant leader Henry of Navarre became heir to the throne in 1584, the League advanced the rival claim of his uncle, the Cardinal of Bourbon [137]. The Leaguers searched French history and law for evidence by which Navarre might be excluded. Many pamphlets between 1585 and 1588 concentrated on the law of succession. Some argued that the Salic law was void, others that the cardinal was the true heir to the throne because of the law of proximity in blood. But there was little that can be considered radical in the writings of the League before May 1588.

The event that unleashed the full force of Leaguer radicalism was the assassination of the Duke of Guise in December 1588 [*Doc. 14*]. On 7 January 1589 the Sorbonne proclaimed that Frenchmen could take up arms against the king, and the Parisian preachers defended regicide from their pulpits. Thus Pierre-François Pigenat, *curé** of St Nicolas-des-Champs, called for the people to avenge the Duke of Guise – the great martyr – in the blood of the hateful tyrant, Henry III. Another priest, Jean Guincestre, said that although he consecrated the host each day, he would not scruple to kill the king. Julien de Moranne, in a pamphlet published in March, recalled that in the Merovingian period a certain Bodillon had killed King Childeric II. 'Will there not be found in France a Bodillon', he asked, 'who will avenge the wrong done ... to a most valiant prince ... by a coward more despicable than Childeric ever was?' [*27 pp. 118–19*].

An important advocate of tyrannicide among the League's propagandists was Jean Boucher, *curé* of St Benoît. As the 'one-eyed king of Paris', he played a leading role in the government of the city from 1589. He was learned in Scripture, canon law and history and was an eloquent preacher, but he frequently resorted to calumny and coarseness. In his *De justa Henrici tertii abdicatione* (August 1589), Boucher argues the case for regarding Henry III as a tyrant, who may be deposed and even killed [*27 pp. 123–44; 103 pp. 97–9*]. He gives little attention to the origin of the state, though he does suggest that kingship is a human institution created by the people for their own convenience. They have transferred sovereignty to the king in a contract between God and the people. The king is bound by this contract, and the people, in order to ensure his observance of its terms, retain power over him. Boucher acknowledges that hereditary succession has become the normal method by which French kings ascend the throne, but he points to the coronation oath as a vestigial reminder of the elective character of the French monarchy. In spite of current appearances, the people still hold the sovereign power. The assemblies of the people can depose a king and wage war against him. Even a private individual has the right of striking down the king who has been declared a tyrant and deposed by one of the institutions of the nation or by the pope. Boucher's discussion of tyrannicide ranges more widely than any Protestant work of the time. He charges Henry III with ten major crimes, each of which is enough to warrant his deposition. It is for the pope, as the supreme judge of Christendom, to release Henry's subjects from their obedience, but even if he does not do so, the people of France must act against the tyrant.

Jacques Clément, the young Dominican friar who assassinated Henry III in August 1589, was undoubtedly influenced by the sermons and polemics which depicted the king as a tyrant and an enemy of the Church [*Doc. 15*]. When news of the assassination reached Paris, Clément was 'canonised' by the League's propagandists. Boucher added a preface and several chapters to his *De justa Henrici tertii abdicatione*. He praises Clément as a martyr for the true faith: 'a new David has killed Goliath; a new Judith has killed Holofernes'. But then he turns briefly to the question of Henry's successor. Brushing aside the candidacy of Henry of Navarre, he calls on the Estates to meet quickly and elect the Cardinal of Bourbon as king. From now on the political writings of the League addressed themselves to the question of the succession. An important contribution to this debate was *De justa reipublicae Christianae in reges impios et haereticos authoritate* (1590), by Gulielmus Rossaeus who has been identified with William Reynolds, an apostate Englishman [27 *pp. 145–60*; 103 *p. 99*; 120 *p. 138*]. It is the most comprehensive treatment of political theory of all the Leaguer writings and comes down heavily on the side of popular sovereignty. Obedience to the king is made to depend on his observing the contract by which he was raised. In particular, he must rule in a Christian manner, and this excludes any heretic from the throne. If he tries to occupy it, he is a tyrant subject to the appropriate penalties. Calvinists, the author contends, are worse than pagans or Turks, and their leader, Henry of Navarre, can never be the 'Most Christian King' of France.

Works defending the Cardinal of Bourbon's right to the throne ceased to be relevant when he died on 9 May 1590. Thereafter each faction in the League advanced its own candidate for the throne.

Mayenne promoted his own claim (there was a revival of arguments used fifteen years earlier tracing the descent of the house of Lorraine from Charlemagne). His nephew, the young duke of Guise, was favoured by most of the Parisian Leaguers, while a group, more vocal than numerous, supported Philip II of Spain or a member of his family. Several Leaguer clerics were, it seems, still imbued with the medieval concept of a *respublica christiana*; they saw nothing wrong in calling on a foreign Catholic prince to save the true faith in France. Among the Sixteen, the death of the Cardinal of Bourbon led to a stronger emphasis being placed on the power of the Estates and of the people. The call for the Estates to elect a Catholic monarch grew loud and insistent [27 *pp. 170–2*].

When Henry of Navarre abjured his Protestant faith in July 1593 he effectively silenced the League's main argument for keeping him off the throne. But his conversion to the Catholic faith could easily be interpreted as an act of political expediency. Among the loudest sceptics was Jean Boucher. Early in August he preached a series of sermons, which were later published under the title *Sermons de la simulée conversion* (March 1594) [27 *pp. 201–7*]. France, he argues, is a Christian state and must have a true Christian ruler, which Navarre, as an excommunicate, cannot be. Despite the pretended absolution at St Denis, Navarre is still a heretic, for bishops cannot absolve someone whom the pope has excommunicated. Even if Henry can prove his sincerity, he is still debarred from the throne under the law of inheritance which excludes permanently anyone who is incapable of inheriting at the time the inheritance is received. Since Henry's conversion is a fraud, the Estates must elect a truly Catholic ruler, even the Spanish Infanta.

It was in December 1593, soon after Henry IV's absolution, that the *Dialogue d'entre le manant et le maheustre* appeared [5] [*Doc. 16*]. Its author was almost certainly François Morin, *sieur* de Cromé, a magistrate in the *Grand Conseil*. The work is in the form of a conversation between a respectable townsman (*manant*) and a nobleman (*maheustre*), and it is also the most radical of the extant Leaguer writings. It not merely expounds the Sixteen's position on the people's right to control the monarch but also delivers a blistering attack on nobles and courtiers. The author, expressing his views through the mouth of the *manant*, prefers the rule of the common people to that of nobles and princes. He comes closer to advocating democracy than any other Leaguer writer. The Sixteen are held up as an example of citizens dedicated to the preservation of the Catholic faith and the liberty of the people. A large part of the *Dialogue* is a history of the Sixteen. The upper classes are blamed for the sufferings of the common people: they have continued the civil wars in France in the hope of seizing more property from the people. The *manant's* attack on the nobility is not aimed at just a few of its members; it is directed at the concept of nobility as it then existed in France. He proposes that hereditary nobility be abolished and that the title of noble be given in acknowledgment of a virtuous life. As for the magistrates of the *Parlement*, they are branded as the ministers of tyranny. The *Parlement* has protected and encouraged heresy, and has betrayed the League. The *manant* is completely disillusioned with the duke of Mayenne and the other noble Leaguers. He is especially angered by Mayenne's opposition to the duke of Guise, who was the choice of the Parisians to succeed to the throne; Mayenne's only concern has been to advance himself.

Following Henry IV's entry into Paris, various measures were taken to stifle the League's propaganda. Death was prescribed for anyone found in possession of seditious books or pamphlets, or who attempted to print them. But on the whole there was little bloodshed, and most of the Parisian Leaguers accepted the new monarch. On 27 December 1594, however, Jean Chastel, a student at the Jesuit college in Paris, tried to assassinate Henry IV [103 *pp. 217–24*]. From his exile in Flanders, Jean Boucher used the occasion to renew his attack on the king. His *Apologie pour Jehan Chastel* (1595) denounced those credulous Catholics who had accepted Henry's conversion as genuine [27 *pp. 222–8*]. The League, he claims, had only opposed tyranny, not the monarchy. In return for defending the true faith it had been branded as seditious. The *Apologie* also sets out to justify Chastel's act. One must not touch the person of a legitimate king, Boucher explains, but the assassination of a tyrant is to be praised. Chastel's purpose was not to kill a king; it was to strike down a usurper. Boucher offers fifteen reasons for distrusting Henry's conversion. He has no right to rule if only because he was excommunicated before his consecration. Not even the pope can restore his right to the throne, nor can the Estates elect him, for he is an outlaw fit only to be executed in public. But the *Apologie* caused little stir in Paris. On 2 April 1594 the Sorbonne and most of the Parisian clergy had formally acknowledged Henry IV as the legitimate king. Many exiles returned and were pardoned, but not Boucher, who died in Flanders in 1646, unnoticed and unmourned.

9 'PARIS IS WORTH A MASS': THE TRIUMPH OF HENRY OF NAVARRE

Although Henry of Navarre had the best claim to succeed Henry III on the French throne, his Protestant faith deterred many Frenchmen from accepting him. As many deserted rather than serve a Protestant monarch, the royal army outside Paris dwindled in size from 40,000 men to 18,000. With such a reduced force Henry could not maintain the siege. He moved to Normandy and the duke of Mayenne followed him there, declaring that he would either throw him into the sea or bring him back to Paris in chains. But on 21 September 1589 Henry defeated Mayenne at Arques near Dieppe [38 *pp. 29–31*]. With the help of English reinforcements Henry made a dash to Paris, but he failed to break through the city's fortifications. So Henry had to retire once again. This time he moved to Tours, where he received the welcome news that Venice had recognised him as king – the first Catholic power to do so [38 *p. 32*].

Instead of going into winter quarters Henry now led a very successful military campaign in Normandy, as a result of which he wrested from the League all the major towns in the province except Rouen and Le Havre. At Ivry, the Leaguers under Mayenne were routed, but Henry was slow to follow up his victory [38 *pp. 32–4*]. The Parisians were able to raise their morale and Henry had to try and starve them into surrender. As the fate of the capital hung in the balance, Philip II of Spain ordered the duke of Parma, his commander in the Netherlands, to lead a diversionary expedition into France. Parma joined Mayenne at Meaux, forcing Henry to withdraw once more. Meanwhile, in the rest of France, the struggle between royalists and Leaguers was fought on largely equal terms.

After his failure to take Paris, Henry was strongly urged by his captains to attack Rouen, the League's main stronghold in northern France, apart from the capital. He did so in November 1591, but a second invasion by Parma forced Henry to abandon the siege of Rouen in April 1592. By the end of the year his main objective – the capture of Paris – seemed as far off as ever. In the provinces the struggle between royalists and Leaguers was dragging on indecisively. If Henry's position was difficult, that of Mayenne was worse. In November 1591 the Sixteen moved against some of the moderates in the Paris *Parlement* and executed three of them [26; 73 *p. 68–9*]. Mayenne had to intervene: he ordered the arrest and execution of the ringleaders and the imprisonment of others of the Sixteen.

Following the death of the Cardinal of Bourbon in May 1590, the various factions within the League failed to agree about his successor as heir to the throne. Some nobles were too busy consolidating their power in the provinces to worry about the king; they merely wanted him to be weak. The same was true of some towns. But Spain wanted an arrangement that would include the Infanta Isabella Clara Eugenia as the wife of a French nobleman. In 1592 Mayenne found himself under pressure from Spain to call a meeting of the Estates-General which, it was hoped, would sanction such an arrangement [85 *p. 216*]. Though hostile to the idea, Mayenne had to give way. In January 1593 the Estates – 128 deputies in all – gathered in Paris [22 *pp. 539–43*]. The duke in his opening address stressed the need to find a Catholic king of France. Henry, for his part, while denying the legal validity of the assembly, suggested talks between its representatives and his own agents. The invitation was bitterly resisted by the more extreme Leaguers, but was accepted by the Estates as a whole. The talks opened at Suresnes on 29 April and a ten-day truce was arranged which was subsequently extended. The only serious obstacle to an agreement was Henry's religion, but on 17 May the archbishop of Bourges announced Henry's decision to become a Catholic again. 'Paris', he is alleged to have remarked, 'is worth a mass'. From the start of his reign he had indicated his willingness to be converted following the deliberations of a 'good, legitimate and free general national council'. Now, in late July 1593, he went to St Denis to receive instruction from a group of prelates and theologians. On 24 July he signed an act of abjuration, and, on the following day, celebrated his change of faith with a masterly display of symbolism. He sent a circular letter to the French provinces announcing his conversion and also wrote to the rulers of Europe to the same effect [131].

Henry's abjuration was the signal for many town governors to declare their loyalty to him. But this also had to be purchased, though the amount paid out in bribes by the king is not precisely known. Estimates vary between 10,714,327 and 6,467,596 *écus* [38

p. 48). Some of the payments may have been intended as compensation for the loss of revenues illegally held from the Crown during the civil wars. Enormous sums were also paid to noblemen, including the dukes of Lorraine, Guise, Mayenne and Nemours and Marshal Joyeuse. Some contemporaries thought that Henry had demeaned the monarchy by making such payments, but, as he told Sully, he would have had to disburse ten times as much to achieve the same results by the sword.

Normally a king of France was crowned at Rheims, but, as this city was still in enemy hands, Henry, relying on several historical precedents, chose Chartres for his coronation. It took place amidst the customary pomp on 27 February 1594. During the ceremony Henry took an oath, promising among other things to 'expel from all lands under my jurisdiction all heretics denounced by the church' [38 p. 50]. In January 1594 Charles, count of Brissac, became Governor of Paris, and he soon plotted to hand over the capital to Henry. The Leaguers and Spain were, it seems, taken completely by surprise. On 22 March royal forces converged on the capital from three directions. The gates were opened from within and the chain across the Seine was lifted. Meeting with little resistance, the royal troops met in the centre of Paris. At six a.m. Henry entered the city and made his way to the cathedral of Notre-Dame, where he attended Mass. Afterwards he watched the departure of the Spanish garrison, and allegedly called out to them: 'My compliments to your master, but do not come back' [22 p. 590].

On 28 March the *Parlement* and the other sovereign courts were re-established; on the 30th a decree cancelled all legislation passed since 29 December 1588 'to the prejudice of the authority of our kings and royal laws'. At Easter Henry demonstrated his orthodoxy by touching 660 people for the King's Evil. Soon afterwards he won over the Sorbonne. In September he reached an agreement with Pope Clement VIII. In return for the pope's absolution, the king promised to recognise the insufficiency of his abjuration, to publish the decrees of the Council of Trent, to restore Catholicism in Béarn and to appoint only Catholics to high office [38 p. 54].

Henry had won control of Paris, but he still needed to rid his kingdom of the Spanish invader. He declared war on Spain in January 1595 and, early in June, moved to Burgundy. At Fontaine-Française, he defeated a Spanish army which had crossed the Alps from Italy to assist the League in Burgundy [22 pp. 610–11]. Mayenne was so disgusted with his allies that he decided to come to terms with Henry. Early in September the king staged a magnificent entry into Lyons. Early in 1596 Mayenne was reconciled to Henry, and Épernon and Joyeuse followed suit. As the young duke of Guise had come over in January, only Mercoeur among the great nobles remained intransigent.

Meanwhile, in northern France, Spain scored a number of successes, culminating in the capture of Amiens in March 1597. News of this disaster galvanised Henry into action. He gathered a large army and laid siege to the city, forcing it to capitulate on 19 September. Early in 1598 Henry advanced into Brittany and imposed a settlement on Mercoeur, who recognised him as king in return for suitable compensation. This marked the end of the League.

THE EDICT OF NANTES, 13 APRIL 1598

It was during his stay in Nantes, Mercoeur's former headquarters, that Henry signed the Edict of Nantes, which regulated his relations with the Huguenots for the rest of his reign [*Doc. 17*]. From the time of his abjuration, Henry's relations with his former co-religionists had seriously deteriorated. Successive Huguenot assemblies at St Foy (1594), Saumur (1595) and Loudun (1596) had witnessed the development of an ever more intransigent group of Protestants. They were so far alienated that in 1597 they refused to assist Henry during the grave crisis that followed the Spanish capture of Amiens. But in April 1598 Henry was strong enough to impose a settlement on the Huguenots. This was the Edict of Nantes, which comprised four separate documents: ninety-two general articles, fifty-six secret articles and two royal warrants [*73 pp. 100–6*].

The purpose of the Edict, as stated in the preamble, was to give all the king's subjects 'a general law, clear, precise and absolute to be applied in all the disputes that have arisen amongst them ... and establish a good and lasting peace'. It gave the Huguenots a large measure of religious toleration. Three categories of Protestant worship were allowed: first, on the estates of noblemen with tenurial rights of justice (*culte privé*); secondly, at two places in each *bailliage* to be determined by royal commissioners (*culte de permission*); and thirdly, wherever the Huguenots could prove that their faith had been openly practised in 1596 and 1597 (*culte de concession*). The Edict made it possible for Huguenots to acquire or inherit any office of state and to enter any profession or occupation. They were granted access to all schools, universities and hospitals. Bi-partisan tribunals (called *chambres de l'édit**) comprising Protestant and Catholic judges were to try lawsuits in which

Huguenots were involved. The secret articles expanded on the general Edict and dealt with exceptions. The two royal warrants were very important as they conferred on the Huguenots a limited military and political independence. The first provided for the payment of Protestant pastors from public funds, and the second set aside an annual sum of 180,000 *écus* over a period of eight years for the payment of garrisons in about fifty Huguenot fortified towns (*places de sûreté*) scattered through western and southern France. The Huguenots were also allowed about 150 emergency forts (*places de refuge*) and eighty other forts which were to be maintained at their own expense.

The Edict of Nantes fell far short of what many Protestants would have liked. It did not put the Huguenot church on the same footing as the Catholic one. The Huguenots could only worship in certain well-defined places. A number of Leaguer cities on surrendering to Henry IV had stipulated that Protestant worship should never be tolerated within their walls. This also applied to all cathedral cities, which is why Protestant churches (called *temples*) had to be built outside the walls in the suburbs. Thus, for instance, Huguenots living in Paris had to go to Charenton to worship. What is more, the Edict called for the restoration of Catholicism wherever it had been suppressed. It provided for the rebuilding of Catholic churches which had been destroyed, the reopening of monasteries and convents, and the restoration of the property of Catholic clergy. Huguenots were expected to stop work on Catholic feast days and to pay tithes to Catholic priests. Protestant books could only be published freely in Huguenot towns; elsewhere they were subject to censorship.

It is also misleading to suggest, as is often done, that the Edict of Nantes created a Huguenot 'state within the state' [127 *p. 371*]. For the two royal warrants on which the claim rests were merely personal promises by Henry IV, which did not bind his successors. Clause 82 of the general articles banned Protestant political assemblies, both national and provincial, thereby disbanding the 'United Provinces of the Midi'. Under the secret articles, colloquies and provincial synods were allowed, but only for religious purposes. Nor was any Huguenot corporation permitted; all Huguenot property had to be individually owned. At best the Edict made the Huguenots a privileged group within the realm, but as compared with many other such estates (e.g. the nobility or clergy) they depended heavily on royal favour and remained on the margins of traditional French society [73 *p. 106*].

To become effective the Edict of Nantes had to be registered by the various *parlements*, and this proved no easy matter, for many Catholics believed that the Edict had given away too much to their opponents. For the first six months of 1598 Henry brought only gentle pressure to bear on the *parlements*. But on 7 February 1599 he called members of the Paris *Parlement* to the Louvre and made a remarkable speech combining entreaty with command [*Doc. 18*]. Three weeks later the *Parlement* registered the Edict, and the other *parlements* then followed suit. Rouen, however, held out till 1609. In the provinces the royal commissioners sent out to enforce the Edict met with resistance from Catholic extremists. The designating of towns where Protestant worship was to be allowed proved difficult, especially in the north and east where Huguenot communities were thin on the ground. The implementation of the Edict was a gigantic task which took years to complete [73 *pp. 106–16*]. Even then constant vigilance had to be applied to the defence of its privileges, which were being continually eroded. Yet overall the Edict can be accounted a success, for open war between Huguenots and Catholics was replaced by cold war. The thousands of lawsuits which came before the *chambres de l'édit* during the seventeenth century bear witness to this: instead of using violence, the opposing parties now resorted to the courts.

Although Henry IV was now officially a Catholic, he welcomed Huguenots to his court and employed them in various public capacities. Ironically, Huguenot architects (e.g. Salomon de Brosse) were largely responsible for Henry's rebuilding of Paris, which had been such a staunch champion of the Catholic cause [113 *pp. 102–3*]. Yet many Huguenots viewed Henry as a traitor to his faith, and Catholics distrusted him for the same reason. All the evidence certainly indicates that his conversion had been the result of political necessity. Catholics also believed, with reason, that the king had failed to fulfil the conditions that had been the price of his absolution by the pope. His foreign policy, too, seems to give the lie to the sincerity of his conversion [103 *pp. 116–38*]. Although he made peace with Spain at Vervins in 1598, he continued to wage a kind of cold war against the Habsburgs till the end of his reign. All this helps to explain why so many attempts were made on the king's life – nineteen in all – before his assassination by a Catholic fanatic in 1610.

The Edict of Nantes, it has been said, 'finally liquidated the religious problem of France' [104 *p. 101*]. Nothing could be further from the truth. Within a short time the civil wars broke out again.

The main reason for this was Louis XIII's decision to apply the Edict in Béarn and to restore Catholicism there. The war, which lasted intermittently for eight years, culminated in the siege and surrender of the Huguenot stronghold of La Rochelle. Under the peace of Alès (1629), the Huguenots lost the military and political guarantees that had been attached to the Edict of Nantes. In October 1685 Louis XIV revoked the Edict of Nantes. He imagined, no doubt, that he had finally liquidated the religious problem of France. But he only succeeded in creating new problems, which necessitated the issue of an Act of Toleration for Protestants in 1797. Only then was the religious problem solved.

PART THREE: ASSESSMENT

10 THE DESTRUCTIVENESS OF THE WARS

POLITICAL EFFECTS

The main political consequence of the Wars of Religion was a drastic diminution of royal authority. Historians have argued at length about the nature of that authority in early sixteenth-century France. It has been described as 'absolute' or 'popular and consultative' [90 *pp. 519–40*]. But everyone agrees that Francis I and Henry II were strongly authoritarian monarchs. If the monarchy was less absolute in the early sixteenth century than it became in the mid-seventeenth, it was certainly tending that way. The king could not be sure that all his wishes would be obeyed, but he commanded the highest respect from his subjects. No one doubted that he was divinely ordained to rule. With the absorption of Brittany into the kingdom and the confiscation of the lands once owned by the Constable of Bourbon, the political unification of France under the Crown was significantly advanced. Various reforms, including the creation of a central treasury (the *Épargne**) improved the efficiency of the administration. Between 1484 and 1560 there was no meeting of the Estates-General, the only national representative body in France: Francis and Henry managed without them. But this situation changed dramatically following the accidental death of Henry II in 1559. His loss underlined the personal nature of monarchy. The replacement of an adult by a child on the throne could have incalculable consequences.

The authority of the monarch in Renaissance France depended to a large extent on the support of the nobility, which still regarded itself as the profession of arms. The most powerful nobles and their sons loved the glory, excitement and material rewards of war. They looked up to a monarch, like Francis I or Henry II, who led his troops into battle. But their martial expectations were dashed by the peace of Cateau-Cambrésis, the death of Henry and the succession to the throne of a boy of fifteen. Under French law, Francis II was old enough to rule, but lacking military or political experience he looked to his kinsmen, the Guises, to administer the kingdom in his name. This caused much offence to many nobles, who regarded the Guises as foreign upstarts without any right to control royal policy. Further resentment was caused by Guise efforts to impose Catholic uniformity by force and to economise by refusing to pay the soldiers returning from Italy.

A year later the crisis deepened as a result of the minority of King Charles IX and the regency of his mother, Catherine de' Medici. Traditionally, a regent in France had less authority than a king who was of age, and a female regent was less respected than a male one. Catherine suffered two additional disadvantages: she was hated as an Italian and despised by some nobles who regarded her as a 'merchant's daughter' [111 *p. 339*]. As respect for the government declined, various aristocratic factions which had been flexing their muscles since the last years of Francis I moved into action. Their aim was to control the person of the king. The Conspiracy of Amboise was an attempt to achieve this by getting rid of the Guises [*Doc. 1*]. In 1562 the Triumvirate succeeded in capturing Charles IX and his mother. Five years later the Huguenots failed in their attempt to kidnap the king at Meaux, but they did not give up their efforts to win him over. Such was the influence of their leader, Coligny, that Catherine de' Medici may have decided to have him murdered rather than allow her son to be drawn into a hazardous armed intervention in the Low Countries. This action precipitated the massacre of St Bartholomew, destroying all Huguenot trust in the Valois dynasty. The Huguenots set up a 'state within the state' south of the Loire and justified their rebellion by advancing the theory that the king owed his authority ultimately to the people [*Docs. 7; 8; 9; 12*].

Whatever Luther and Calvin once said about the need to obey the divinely instituted ruler, the Huguenots refused to believe that God was a party to their persecution. Consequently, they decided to govern themselves until such time as the crown could be placed on a responsible head. Thus politics combined with religion to undermine the material and theoretical foundations of the French monarchy. Under Henry III, the Catholic extremists, disenchanted with the king's attempts to win back the Huguenots through religious concessions, formed their own autonomous Catholic League. The crisis was made worse by the childlessness of the king which opened the way to the throne for the Huguenot leader, Henry of Navarre. Fearing a Protestant succession, the League backed an alternative candidate, justifying its action by means of political theories even more radical than those previously used by its Huguenot opponents.

In 1588 Henry III tried to free himself from the League by murdering its leader, the duke of Guise [*Doc. 14*]. The effect of this crime was almost as grave as that of the massacre of St Bartholomew, for it drove the League into open rebellion, which culminated in Henry's own assassination [*Doc. 15*]. This perhaps marked the nadir of the monarchy before the French Revolution, for no French king had yet been murdered by one of his subjects.

The decline of the French monarchy in the second half of the sixteenth century was reflected in two important administrative areas: local government and taxation. Pre-eminent among the officers of the Crown, who exercised its authority at the level of the localities, were the provincial governors. These were usually great noblemen, who were given special responsibility for the defence of their respective areas. Under Francis I and Henry II they seldom resided in their provinces, being more often at court or in the king's armies in Italy or elsewhere, for most of them were captains in the *compagnies d'ordonnance**, units of heavily armoured cavalry which formed the nucleus of the French army. The essential link between a governor and his province was provided by the clientage system. He gained the loyalty and obedience of the province by defending its interests at court and by acting as a broker in the dispensing of royal gifts to its inhabitants [74 *pp. 31–7*].

After the peace of Cateau-Cambrésis, however, the governors were instructed to reside in their provinces and to impose order on the soldiers who returned home for the first time in many decades. The governors were suddenly able to dispose of considerable locally based forces, and they began to display their power by travelling about with huge armed escorts. Thus the Prince of Condé had an escort of 500 noblemen in 1560, and the Governor of Languedoc turned up at Fontainebleau with 800. Such a militarisation of provincial society constituted a threat to royal authority, but this only became a reality when the governors found that they could no longer rely on promoting the interests of their clients at court. In the 1560s royal patronage was either severely curtailed or restricted to clients of the Guises. A governor who suffered as a result was Louis de Bourbon, duke of Montpensier. 'He is so little respected', he complained, 'in all the requests he makes for his clients that he never obtains anything although he has sought things given to others; this completely discredits him and disheartens many in his service who get no other recompense than that which comes from M. de Montpensier's own funds' [74 *pp. 48–9*]. Similar complaints were made by other governors at the time.

Inevitably some clients, finding that they could no longer depend on their patrons, turned to alternative sources of support and advancement. Such an alternative was provided by the new Calvinist churches, which were seeking armed protection from their persecutors. Thus it was reported from Guyenne in 1560 that disaffected nobles were deserting their leaders for the new religion. 'They colour their actions with religion', wrote Biron, 'saying that they had put too much faith in men and must put their faith in Him' [74 *p. 49*]. As France slipped into civil war, the governors were also angered by the lack of clear and decisive instructions from the central government as to how the Huguenots should be treated. Marshal Tavannes, for example, 'received different dispatches from court: those from the Guise said to kill them all; those from the queen said to save them all' [74 *p. 54*]. Such confusion naturally encouraged the governors to act as they thought best. In the face of imminent danger several of them began to form local political associations. Some were aristocratic vigilante organisations, like the Flassans of Provence, who were set up in 1561 to attack Calvinist assemblies. Others had a wider social basis, such as the association formed in Toulouse in 1563 'for the defence of the Catholic religion'. Soon there were religious associations under governors all over southern France, which owed nothing to the Crown. One of them was described by de Bèze as 'a veritable conspiracy of public powers against the royal will' [74 *p. 58*]. The most independent of the provincial governors was Henri de Montmorency-Damville, son of the old Constable, who in 1574 assumed the leadership of the Huguenots and *politiques* of Languedoc. Though he was denounced as a rebel and replaced by another governor, he was never actually removed and, in 1577, resumed his allegiance to the Crown after his pension had been increased. Bribery was one method used by the Crown to control the governors, but this was in itself an admission of royal weakness. Henry III showed that he was aware of the dangerous powers exercised by the provincial governors when he issued the famous Ordinance of Blois (May 1579). This prescribed a reduction in the number of governors and ordered them not to appropriate royal prerogatives, such as granting pardons, borrowing money, authorising markets and fairs, and levying taxes [130 *p. 172*]. But like so much of Henry's legislation, this remained a dead letter.

The effectiveness of a political régime can be measured by its ability to raise sufficient revenue for its needs. This never happened in sixteenth-century France. The taxation system was riddled with anomalies and only a small proportion of the revenues collected ever reached the central treasury. In order to pay for their wars Francis I and Henry II had to supplement their regular income from taxation, direct and indirect, by resorting to expedients, such as loans, alienations of crown lands, *rentes**, sales of titles of nobility and of offices* [90 *pp. 188–91*]. In spite of such methods they failed to meet their obligations, leaving their successors a large debt that was compounded by the Price Revolution (see below p. 91). One of the first actions of Francis II's government was to try to bring the Crown's finances under control. In an attempt to economise, the Guises dismissed officials and troops, reduced pensions, cut down on gifts to nobles and set about recovering alienated crown lands. Such a policy aroused the hatred of many soldiers and courtiers, yet savings alone could not bridge the gap between royal income and expenditure. At the Estates-General of 1560 the Chancellor, Michel de l'Hôpital, confirmed that royal debts totalled 43 million *livres*. He asked for higher taxes, but the deputies would not oblige. At Pontoise, in 1561, however, the clergy did make a substantial contribution by agreeing to pay the Crown a 'voluntary' subsidy totalling 22.6 million *livres* over sixteen years. In 1563 Catherine de' Medici succeeded in forcing through an alienation of church lands, an operation that was repeated on a number of subsequent occasions. It has been estimated that between 1561 and 1587 such sales brought the king a total of 20 million *livres* [130 *pp. 126–9*]. But the Crown used this money to float new *rentes* rather than to settle the interest on old ones. This became a major grievance among the *rentiers** of Paris in the 1580s.

A much-criticised expedient used by the Crown throughout the Wars of Religion was the sale of offices (venality). As Bodin said in 1566, tyrants 'think up new offices and honours, and offer these for a price, that they may have many bound to them. They appoint thieves and criminals for public office, and for the collection of revenue, so that they sap the people's resources and blood' [130 *p. 129*]. The rulers themselves admitted that venality interfered with good government: the Edict of Orléans (1561) promised to abolish it, yet it constantly increased in scope and importance. Under the system of *alternatif** (created in 1554, abolished under Francis II and restored in 1568) certain offices were sold twice, the holders serving in alternate years. Venality was so much abused in the late sixteenth century that towns, parishes, *bailliages* and *élections** were at times blanketed with additional office-holders.

The Crown might have been less dependent on expedients if only it had been sure of receiving all the regular taxes it levied. But during the Wars of Religion much of that money was diverted into other purses. A town under siege, for example, would not hesitate to use local revenues to buy off the enemy or to shore up its defences. During the first civil war town magistrates in large areas of France under Huguenot control used royal revenues to pay Condé's troops. In predominantly Catholic areas the Huguenots seized the royal cash boxes. Condé also levied taxes on his own authority and even, in some cases, authorised the minting of coins. All of these appropriations of royal revenue deserved to be punished, but the Crown was too weak. Under the Peace of Amboise, Condé was 'absolved for all the moneys which, by him and on his commandment and ordinance, have been seized and levied from our treasuries and revenues, for whatever sums to which these may amount' [130 *p. 145*]. Other Huguenots were also pardoned for similar offences, not once but in every pacification, including the Edict of Nantes. Thus rebels were able to pay for their war effort out of the king's own revenues. After the massacre of St Bartholomew, virtually the entire royal tax machine in southern France was taken over by the Huguenots. In 1575 the Venetian ambassador asked, 'How can there ever be peace in the realm, since it is the plain truth that for its own gain [each faction] stands ready to foment war? ... Thus where the king spends thousands in the fighting, they spend nothing – at least nothing of their own, but rather of others and of the king. And while the king destroys himself, they, on the contrary, pile up their holdings, holdings they would lose if peace were to come, as they would lose their power and following, with the danger that these might never return again' [130 *pp. 151–2*].

Henry III was plagued with financial problems throughout his reign [33 *pp. 23–9*]. The cost of war was rising all the time, yet he could not persuade his subjects to give him more money. They suspected that he would merely squander it on his favourites, and they had grounds for thinking this. The king apparently offered a wedding gift of 1.2 million *livres* to Épernon, which the latter allegedly declined on the ground that the royal finances were too heavily burdened. Whatever the truth may have been, Henry certainly found himself in desperate straits: since his subjects would not trust him, he was reduced to begging, pawning his jewels and borrowing. Without the support of the Italian bankers, his government might well have foundered, but in return for their loans they demanded control of the most lucrative taxes. Henry III, it has been claimed, has been much maligned by historians [34; 40; 45]. Certainly he was an intelligent monarch and he had reason to be sincerely interested in administrative reform. The Ordinance of Blois (May 1579) was prompted in part by signs of resistance to royal taxes in many areas, but it promised more than it could deliver. Thus an undertaking to reduce the *taille** was not implemented, so that at the Estates-General of 1588 the deputies complained that the tax had actually doubled since 1579. The archbishop of Bourges warned the king that France was 'a sick body which had been too much bled' [130 *p. 181*]. After the murder of the duke of Guise, the tax system was widely plundered by the king's enemies. In Burgundy and Champagne, for example, the duke of Mayenne imposed taxes as if he were the king. Indeed, the Burgundian estates complained in 1591 that they were paying more to the duke than they had ever done to the king. Another nobleman who appropriated royal revenues was the duke of Nevers. Elsewhere towns found it convenient to use royal taxes for their own purposes. More or less everywhere the fiscal administration was reduced to chaos, yet its essential components survived. What saved it from destruction was the accession of Henry of Navarre, who was able to re-integrate into the kingdom the so-called 'United Provinces of the Midi'.

SOCIAL AND ECONOMIC EFFECTS

To assess the effects of the religious wars on the economy and society of sixteenth-century France is no easy task, for the wars coincided with a period of economic crisis which they helped to exacerbate. An important element of the crisis can be traced back to around the year 1540, when a gap began to appear between the population of France and her food supply. From at least the beginning of the century the population had been rising steadily, yet the amount of food that was being produced failed to keep pace with this rise. The reason for this shortfall was essentially technological backwardness within the agricultural sector, notably in respect of fertilising the soil. But other factors were also at work. Much depended on the quality of the harvests, which was determined by the weather. A harsh winter followed by a wet summer could easily wipe out the harvest for one year, and this would tilt the precarious balance between survival and extinction that existed in the life of the average peasant. A single bad harvest was bad enough, but two or three in succession would produce a famine comparable to the kind that regularly hits the Third World today. Famine alone could easily cause deaths on a large scale, particularly among the poor and the old, and because it undermined human resistance to disease it could also pave the way to plague and other infectious diseases.

On top of all this was the inflation that is commonly called 'the Price Revolution' – a rise in prices which affected the whole of western Europe in the sixteenth century. In the past this was commonly ascribed to the importation of silver, and to a lesser extent gold, into Europe from America. But it had other causes as well: notably, the rising population, the huge expenditure on war by various governments, and coinage depreciation. By pushing up the price of foodstuffs and other necessities, inflation helped to worsen the lot of ordinary people, whose wages (if they were paid at all) did not keep abreast of prices.

The start of the Wars of Religion also roughly coincided with a change in the climate of western Europe. Historians of climate, using evidence supplied by Alpine glaciers, tree-rings and vintage charts, have detected a tendency towards colder winters starting around 1560 and continuing till the mid-nineteenth century. They have called it 'the Little Ice Age', though in fact the alteration in the mean temperature was very small [111 *p. 355–7*]. But even this could be disastrous to a population heavily dependent on vegetable and cereal crops for employment, food and drink. Contemporary records show that there were very harsh winters in France in 1565, 1568, 1570 and 1573. In Paris the winter of 1565, followed by a wet summer, led to a 400 per cent rise in grain prices in July. The cold spring of 1573 destroyed crops on such a scale that many peasants converged on the towns in search of food. In 1595 the price of a measure of wheat (*setier*) on the Paris market rose to 25 *livres* as against 15 in 1574 and 8 in 1572. A drought in the summer of 1583 caused many deaths among the poor in Lyons during the following winter. Crops, of course, varied from one province to another, and ideally it should have been possible to organise some form of mutual aid, but the desire to assist a neighbour in need was seldom strong enough to overcome the logistical difficulties presented by poor communications and lack of transport. Famine became widespread in the 1590s.

Famine often paved the way for plague, which assumed a new virulence in France during the civil wars, particularly after 1577 [73 *pp. 162–3*]. In Rouen, Beauvais, Amiens and Paris there were outbreaks of plague during the first civil war. One of the most serious plagues of the century occurred in 1586–87. In Rouen famine and plague joined forces in 1586 with terrible results. Grain prices rocketed to the highest levels in living memory and attempts to alleviate the food shortage by importing rye from the Baltic area were hampered by English privateers. At least sixteen ships laden with rye from Danzig were intercepted and taken to England. The result was a serious mortality in Rouen. An English observer reported: '... they dye in evrie streete and at evrie gate, morning and eveninge, by viii or xii in a place, so that the like hath not byne heard of. And the poore doth not onely die so in the streete, but the riche also in their bedde by 10 or 12 in a daye' [30 *p. 173*]. Parish records show that the city's gravediggers worked more than twice as fast as usual in 1586–87. According to L'Estoile, 30,000 Parisians died of plague in the summer of 1580. Nor was plague the only infectious disease at the time: malaria and smallpox were rife, and in 1580 there was a kind of influenza, called the *coqueluche*, which claimed many victims.

Two important facts need to be remembered when judging the effects of the Wars of Religion in France. First, they were not continuous: although they lasted officially from 1562 till 1598, thirteen years of peace or relative peace intervened between those dates. Secondly, the wars did not hit every region of France equally hard. Some areas – notably, Normandy, the Loire valley, Poitou and Auvergne – saw a great deal of fighting, while others (e.g. Brittany and Béarn) saw comparatively little. It is consequently difficult to generalise about the effects of the wars. Yet by and large the wars caused much hardship in the countryside and in the towns. In both economic activity was severely disrupted, for soldiers in the sixteenth century were expected to live off the land, and their greed was often made worse by the fact that they were poorly paid or not paid at all. They would requisition food and forage from the peasants without concern for the delicate balance between survival and starvation. They would ruin the forthcoming harvest by stripping the fields of corn prematurely and feeding it to their horses. Pillaging by soldiers was an everyday event: they would steal grain, horses and cattle from the peasant, rape his wife and daughters, and try to extort money from him by torturing his children. Countless villages were put to ransom, houses set on fire, fruit trees cut down and vines uprooted. Some of the worst offenders were the foreign mercenaries, mainly German *reiters** and *landsknechts**, who would systematically lay waste a whole area through which they passed and carry off huge quantities of booty and large herds of cattle. Claude Haton, a priest from Provins (Brie), has left us vivid descriptions of the horrors of war in his part of the country. His account of the troops assembled by Anjou in 1578 needs no comment: 'they were all vagabonds, thieves, and murderers – men who renounced God along with all the worldly debts they owed. These slaughtermen were the flotsam of war, riddled with the pox and fit for the gibbet. Dying of hunger, they took to the roads and fields to pillage, assault, and ruin the people of the towns and villages, who fell into their clutches in the places where they lodged' [9 p. 937; 119 pp. 207–8]. Can one wonder that the peasants, on hearing of the approach of an army, would commonly abandon their daily pursuits and take to the woods and forests? Such an exodus would, of course, further disrupt food production.

The hardships suffered by the peasantry as a result of the activities of unruly soldiers were bound sooner or later to provoke a response. This happened in the Vivarais, for example, where a peasant revolt broke out in 1575 [120 pp.211–34]. Ostensibly it was a tax revolt, but it was really directed at the garrisons for which the tax was being levied. In February 1579 the peasants sent a petition to the king listing all the atrocities committed against them by 'the *gentilshommes*, captains and soldiers'. In a single year, they claimed, the impositions placed upon them, first by the Catholic, then by the Protestant garrisons, had exceeded the amount of the *taille* in thirty years. They asked for a special court to rid the countryside of the 'vermin' of soldiery. At times the exasperation of the peasants expressed itself in violence against their social superiors. Thus in Brittany in September 1590 a wedding party, including some sixty nobles, was completely wiped out by a band of armed peasants. But the most important peasant uprising was the revolt of the Croquants, which began in 1593 and soon spread to a large part of western France. Most contemporary observers saw its main cause as the cruelties and illegal extortions of the nobility, but it was not directed against the nobility as such. In the words of J.H.M. Salmon: 'it was not the normal administration of the seigneurial regime, but rather its gross abuse in circumstances of civil anarchy, that provoked the risings. The plight of the peasantry was the result of three decades of civil war' [119 p. 282]. The poet d'Aubigné despised the Croquants, but he was not insensitive to their suffering. In his *Les Tragiques* he describes the plight of a wounded and starving peasant of Périgord who had witnessed the slaughter of his wife and children and had been left to die by the soldiers. Henry IV showed sympathy for the cause of the peasants. He allegedly said that if he had not been born to inherit the Crown, he would have been a Croquant [119 *p. 285*].

If the countryside suffered grievously during the Wars of Religion, the towns also had to face terrible hardships. They too were visited by famines and epidemics, and many were directly caught up in the fighting, for sieges became an important aspect of military strategy on both sides. While a town was under siege its economic activity was largely curtailed, if it was not brought to a halt altogether. If a town was taken by storm, it was usually sacked; if it surrendered, it often had to pay a large ransom. But surrender did not necessarily avert a sack. Issoire, for example, was sacked in June 1577 even though it had capitulated. As de Thou noted: 'most of the town and all its riches were reduced to cinders'. Rouen was never treated so harshly, but its day-to-day life was much disrupted by the wars [30]. In 1562 it was taken over by the Huguenots, then besieged, recaptured and sacked by royal forces in October. Even after the first civil war had ended, Rouen's overseas trade was regularly harassed by English, Dutch and Rochelais corsairs. In 1572 the city was the scene of one of the worst of the St Bartholomew's Day massacres. But the crowning blow was the struggle between Henry IV and the Catholic League after 1589, which brought troops back to the region in large numbers for five years. Between November 1591 and April 1592 the city was again besieged by royal forces. One of the worst sieges of the civil wars was the siege of Paris in 1590, during which many of the inhabitants died of starvation, as Henry IV held many of the towns that normally supplied the capital with grain and other provisions [38 *pp. 35–6*].

The civil wars greatly affected the commercial life of France, but they cannot be entirely blamed for all its vicissitudes. Nor was the situation one of unrelieved decline. Some cities were badly affected while others continued to prosper. As always in sixteenth-century France, there were marked regional variations. The fortunes of Lyons and Marseilles may be taken as an example. In the first half of the century Lyons had enjoyed a period of unprecedented prosperity [44; 71]. Its four annual fairs had attracted merchants from far and wide, and its banks, mainly run by Italians, had conducted much profitable business. But the situation underwent a change before the outbreak of the wars. In 1551 a monetary crisis caused several bankruptcies. In 1557 the failure of the *Grand Parti*** shook many banking houses and the traders dependent on them. But it was the Huguenot takeover of the city in April 1562 which spelt economic disaster, for the fairs had to be moved first to Montluel, then to Chalon-sur-Saône. Business recovered in the years 1564 to 1570, but as the civil war spread in the 1570s Lyons found some of its essential supply routes cut off by roving war bands. At the same time the wars aggravated an existing monetary crisis [44 *pp. 326–8*]. Silver had by now taken the place of gold as the principal bullion import from America. As gold became scarce, bankers asked to be paid in gold. The gold *écu au soleil* circulated freely at a rate higher than that which was officially quoted. Traders asked for their debts to be expressed in gold *écus*, not in *livres tournois*, and to protect themselves from any depreciation in respect of silver, they pushed up their prices. A royal ordinance of September 1577 ordered all accounts to be in *écus* instead of *livres*, but this provided only a brief respite along the inflationary road. As monetary confidence weakened, trade became depressed. There was a sharp fall in the yield from duties on goods entering Lyons. The famous silk industry went into recession for the first time, and the cloth industry, one of the most important in France, failed to compete effectively with a flood of English cloth which entered the kingdom. For a time the Lyons bankers weathered the storm, but after 1572 many went bankrupt. A number moved their businesses to Paris, which seemed to offer better prospects.

Lyons' troubles were not necessarily repeated elsewhere. Marseilles, by contrast, enjoyed a boom during the civil wars, in spite of its former dependence on Lyons for financial support [44 *pp. 328–9*]. The Cyprus war, by drawing the Venetians away from the Levant, enabled the Marseillais to take advantage of concessions they had received from the Sultan Selim II in 1569. They took over the spice trade and their success can be seen from the steep rise in the yield of harbour dues at Marseilles: from 7,000 to 8,000 *livres* in 1570, to 12,000 in 1571, 15,000 in 1572 and 19,000 in 1573. But the boom was short-lived, for the Marseillais soon had to face severe Anglo-Dutch competition in the Mediterranean.

What impact did the civil wars have on the population of France? A satisfactory answer to this question is impossible, since the documentary evidence available is at best patchy. It consists of a few baptismal registers and some fiscal records. Any estimate of the total population of France in the sixteenth century can only be an inspired guess. According to one expert it was between 16 and 18 million in 1600 [111 *p. 363*]. But everyone is agreed that France was the most populous country in western Europe in 1500, and that her population rose steadily from the late fifteenth century onwards. Even during the civil wars it seems that the upward trend continued.

In fact, demographic historians have tended in recent years to minimise the effects of the wars. For instance, Goubert has stated that they 'in no way seriously hindered the general upward movement of baptisms ... provided we disregard the ten years 1590–9' [154 *p. 465*]. Another scholar, Richet, has argued that the growth may have been checked by the 1560s in the Midi, but that it continued in the north for at least two decades after 1562 [185]. However, the evidence of town records points in a different direction. According to Benedict, the population of Rouen fell by more than a quarter between 1562 and 1594 [138 *p. 232*]. This was not necessarily due to mortality; emigration has also to be taken into account, for many Protestants left the city to avoid persecution. At first they settled in Geneva; later (after the massacre of St Bartholomew) they went to England. Some of these exiles returned to Rouen under Henry IV, when the city's population recovered to a level only 5 to 15 per cent below the pre-civil war era. Deaths during the civil wars were not always caused by fighting: famine and disease took a heavy toll. It was mainly in the last fifteen or twenty years of the century that the population fell, especially in the towns. Allowing for a wide margin of error and for considerable regional variations, one can perhaps estimate the total fall in population during the wars at between 2 and 4 million [111 *p. 363*].

RECOVERY?

It is commonly assumed that once Henry IV had abjured Protestantism, conceded the Edict of Nantes to his former co-religionists, and appointed the duke of Sully as his finance minister, all the problems that had divided and ruined France in the previous half-century were solved. But we must beware of the myth created around Henry following his assassination in 1610. A share of responsibility for that myth must be borne by Sully, who, following his retirement from public life in 1611, wrote a book – the *Économies royales* – in which he greatly exaggerated the king's achievement and his own.

A measure of recovery certainly did take place under Henry IV, for which Sully deserves a share of the credit. By 1610 he had accumulated perhaps as much as 15 million *livres* in the king's coffers, but he only managed this by operating an undeclared bankruptcy. He defaulted on Henry's debts to his foreign allies (e.g. England and the Dutch), and he abandoned the payment of arrears of *rentes*. By 1605 these stood at nineteen years in certain cases [33 *pp. 54–8*]. Essentially the surplus on the current account was achieved by cutting expenditure and maximising revenues rather than by any thorough-going reforms. A return to economic prosperity resulted in an increased yield from indirect taxes which were also more effectively administered. A regular income from the sale of offices was ensured by the creation of the *droit annuel** or *Paulette**, a tax of one-sixtieth of the value of the office, which enabled the holder to dispose of it freely. By 1610 the income from this source accounted for 12 per cent of ordinary revenues. Financiers were also squeezed: in 1601 Sully forced them to disgorge 600,000 *livres*. In 1607 he asked them for 1.2 million, though it is not certain how much he actually got.

So there was undoubtedly an improvement in the Crown's financial situation after 1598; but the damage inflicted by the Wars of Religion on the king's authority could not be repaired overnight. Even after peace with Spain had been signed (April 1598), the great nobles remained troublesome. The reign of Henry IV was punctuated by aristocratic plots (the duke of Biron, 1602; Balzac d'Entragues, 1604; the duke of Bouillon, 1602–6; the Prince of Condé, 1609). The king had to pay heavily to secure the loyalty of the rest. Sully estimated that he spent between 30 and 32 million *livres* in treaties 'for the recovery of the kingdom', though it seems that he did not always honour them. As Sir George Carew commented: 'those, who hazarded their lives and fortunes for settling the crown upon his head, [the king] neither rewardeth nor payeth; those, who were of the League against him, he hath bought to be his friends and giveth them preferments' [33 *p. 43*]. To raise the money for such bribes, Henry had to put pressure on the traditional tax-payers, mainly the peasantry, at a time of economic hardship. He also had to disappoint the *rentiers* and the office-holders, who had looked to him as the candidate for the throne most likely to bring them peace and to improve their lot. In 1595 the office-holders complained that he had let them down.

As for the religious problem, this too survived the Edict of Nantes. Although this was officially described as 'perpetual' and irrevocable', it was never intended as a permanent settlement. A phrase in the Edict clearly points to its temporary nature: 'God has not seen fit that my subjects should *as yet* worship and adore Him under one form of religion'. This view was shared by Catholics and Huguenots, who both regarded the Edict as an unfortunate necessity. Each side was convinced that, given time, it would convert the other. In many ways the Edict was a success. Unlike former pacifications it lasted for eighty-seven years, but it did not place the two religions on an equal footing. It gave security to the Protestant communities, but it circumscribed their influence by preventing them from proselytising.

At the same time, many Huguenot nobles adopted the king's religion out of self-interest. Thus the Huguenot communities lost much of their leadership. Geographically too they became more circumscribed. After 1598 more than 80 per cent of Huguenots lived in western, and above all, southern France. They concentrated their energies on defending their privileges under the Edict, which were being constantly eroded. 'The militant dynamic of the sixteenth century gave way to concentration on survival and self-defence. Open war was replaced by cold war' [113 *p. 287*].

PART FOUR: DOCUMENTS

All the ensuing documents, except nos 8, 9, 12, 17 and 18, are in the author's own translations.

THE TUMULT OF AMBOISE, 1560

Historians have argued at length about whether or not the Tumult of Amboise was a Calvinist plot to overthrow the government of the Guises. This contemporary description blames a mixture of motives for the failure of the plot. It is taken from the Histoire ecclésiastique des églises réformées au royaume de France, *published in Antwerp in 1580. Its 3,000 pages deal with the history of the Huguenot churches from 1521 to 1577. It was once attributed to Calvin's lieutenant, de Bèze, but is now thought to have been compiled under his supervision from reports sent to him by many congregations throughout France. Despite its polemical character the work throws valuable light on the formative stages of the Huguenot churches.*

These openly tyrannical practices, the threats used on this occasion against the highest in the kingdom, the setting aside of the princes and great lords, the contempt for the Estates of the realm, the corruption of the principal judges and their devotion to the new governors [the Guises], the finances of the kingdom squandered by their command on anyone they liked along with all the offices and benefices; in short, their violent and in itself unlawful government aroused great hatred of them and caused several noblemen to awaken as from a deep sleep. In their view the two kings, Francis and Henry, had never wanted to attack the persons of men of estate, being content to hunt the dog rather than the wolf, yet exactly the opposite was taking place when it was necessary (if only because of their number) to use less corrosive remedies and to avoid opening the gates to countless seditions. Each one, then, was driven to look to his own interest, and several began to meet in order to find a just form of defence and a way to restore the old and lawful government of the kingdom. Jurists and other eminent persons in France and Germany were consulted as well as the most learned theologians, and it was established that one could lawfully oppose the government usurped by the Guises and even take up arms if necessary to repulse their violence, provided the princes of the blood (who are lawful magistrates by right of birth in such cases), or one of them, are prepared to do so, especially if requested by the Estates of France or the better part thereof. To approach the king and his council would have been tantamount to warning the enemy, for the king (his minority apart) had become their slave, so that it was impossible to bring them to trial in the normal way. As for the queen-mother, she seemed merely to shadow their activities. Thus it was necessary to seize their persons by any means and then to call the Estates so as to force them to account for their administration. Once this course of action had been decided by common consent, three kinds of people took the matter in hand: the first were moved by zeal to serve God, their prince and fatherland; the second by ambition and desire for change; and the third were spurred on by thirst of vengeance for the outrages committed by the Guises against themselves, their kinsmen and allies. Thus it is not to be wondered at that there was confusion and that the affair ended in tragedy.

Histoire ecclésiastique, [2], vol. 1, pp. 285–6.

DOCUMENT 2   MICHEL DE L'HÔPITAL: THE VOICE OF MODERATION, 13 DECEMBER 1560

Michel de l'Hôpital was appointed Chancellor of France on 1 April 1560. He had risen to power with the help of the Guises, but, on achieving his high office, he tried to steer a neutral course and urged Frenchmen to seek a peaceful solution of their religious differences. Here is an extract from his opening speech to the Estates-General of Orléans on 13 December 1560.

It is said that the other main cause of sedition is religion, which is strange and wellnigh incredible; for if sedition is bad; if, as Thucydides says, it comprises every sort of evil, how can religion, if it is good, engender evil and produce an effect contrary to its nature? What is more, if sedition is the same as civil war, which is worse than foreign war, how can it be caused by the Christian and evangelical faith, which prescribes above all peace and friendship among men? *Non enim dissensionis, sed pacis author Deus* [for God is the author, not of strife, but of peace]. And if this religion is Christian, those who try to spread it by using arms, swords and pistols act against their belief, which is to suffer violence, not to inflict it. In this respect, says Chrysostom, we differ from the Gentiles who use force and constraint; Christians use words and persuasion.

Their argument that they take up arms in God's cause is worthless; for God's cause cannot be defended with arms. *Mitte gladium tuum in vaginam* [Sheath your sword in its scabbard]. Our religion did not spring from arms.

If it were said that the arms they use are for self-defence, not to attack others, this might be valid in respect of a foreigner, but not of the king, their sovereign lord; for it is no more permitted for the subject to defend himself against the prince or magistrates than for the son to do so against his father, regardless of right and wrong, of the wickedness or goodness of the prince or magistrate. We are bound to obey the prince even more than the father ...

It is true that if men were good and perfect they would never take up arms for the sake of religion; yet it cannot be denied that religion, good or bad, can arouse men's passions more than anything else. It is madness to hope for peace, repose and friendship among persons of different religion. No belief penetrates more deeply into the hearts of men than religion or divides them more widely from each other ... We experience this to-day and see that a Frenchman and an Englishman sharing the same faith are closer in love and friendship than are two Frenchmen of the same city, subject to the same lord, who have different faiths. Whereas religious unity transcends national unity, religious division separates more than any other. It divides father from son, brother from brother, husband from wife. *Non veni pacem mittere sed gladium* [I have not come to send peace but a sword]. It deters the subject from obeying his king and produces rebellion ...

For this reason we must remove the cause of the evil and provide a remedy by means of a council, as was recently suggested at Fontainebleau and of which the pope has given us hope in response to the urgent request of the late King Francis. Meanwhile, gentlemen, let us obey our young king. Let us not take up new opinions too hastily, each in his own way. Let us think carefully first and educate ourselves; for what is at stake is no trifling matter: it is the salvation of our souls. For if it is allowable for each of us to adopt a new faith at will, then be prepared to see as many kinds of faith as there are families and leaders of men. Your religion, you say, is better than mine; I defend mine. Which is the more reasonable way: that I should follow your opinion or you mine? Who will judge if it is not a sacred council?

Let us not be careless; let us not bring war into the kingdom through sedition or disturb and confuse everything. I promise you that the king and queen will do everything to bring about a council, and, if this remedy fails, they will resort to other means used by their predecessors ... If the decline of our church has given birth to heresies, then its reformation may serve to extinguish them. We have behaved so far like bad captains who attack the enemy's fort with all their might but leave their own homes undefended. We must henceforth ... assail our enemies with charity, prayer, persuasion and the word of God, which are the proper weapons for such a conflict ... Sweetness will achieve more than severity. And let us banish those devilish names – 'Lutheran', 'Huguenot', 'Papist' – which breed only faction and sedition; let us retain only one name: 'Christian'.

Michel de l'Hôpital, [13] vol. 1, pp. 394–402.

DOCUMENT 3   THE COLLOQUY OF POISSY,
9 SEPTEMBER–18 OCTOBER 1561

At the end of August 1561 Théodore de Bèze, who had been chosen as the
Protestant spokesman, arrived in France from Geneva. Here is part of his
account of the Colloquy of Poissy.

About noon on 9 September there gathered at Poissy, in the large refectory
of the nuns, the king with, on the right of the hall looking across its width,
his brother the duke of Orléans and the king of Navarre, and, on the left,
the queen-mother and the queen of Navarre. Behind them were many
princes and princesses, knights of the order, lords and nobles, and ladies of
every quality. On either side of the hall, looking along its length, sat three
cardinals with, beneath them, thirty-six bishops and archbishops, and,
behind them, a huge crowd of ecclesiastics, theologians, representing clergy
of every kind and degree. Opposite the king stood his guard and a sizeable
group of people of all estates. Once they had been silenced, the king spoke
as follows:

'*Messieurs*, I have summoned you from various parts of my kingdom so
that you may advise me on what my chancellor will propose to you. I beg
you to set aside all prejudice so that we may achieve something which will
bring peace to my subjects, honour to God, the salving of consciences and
public tranquillity. I desire this so much that I have decided to keep you
here until you have reached a settlement that will enable my subjects to live
in unity and peace with each other, as I trust you will do. By acting thus
you will make it possible for me to protect you as my royal predecessors
have done.'

The twelve ministers and twenty-two representatives of the provincial
churches who assisted them were then called and presented by the duke of
Guise, as was his duty, and by the *sieur* de la Ferté, captain of the guard.
They were led to the bar against which they leant, bareheaded. Théodore de
Bèze, who had been elected as their mouthpiece, spoke as follows:

'Sire, since the success of any enterprise great or small depends on God's
help and favour, especially when the issue at stake concerns His service and
transcends our understanding, we hope that Your Majesty will not be
offended or surprised if we start with the following prayer: "Lord God,
eternal and all-powerful Father, we confess and acknowledge before Your
sacred Majesty that we are poor, wretched sinners, conceived and born in
sin and corruption, inclined to evil, incapable of good, and that our
sinfulness causes us to break your sacred commandments continually and
endlessly: thus we fairly deserve by your judgment ruin and damnation".'
[De Bèze then gave an account of Calvin's doctrine.]

This speech satisfied the whole assembly, as some of its most difficult and
awkward members have since admitted. It was listened to with close
attention until de Bèze had nearly finished speaking of the Real Presence of
Jesus Christ in the Last Supper. Although, he explained, the body of Christ

is truly offered and communicated to us therein, it is as far removed from the bread as are the heavens from the earth. This caused the prelates to stir and murmur, although he had said much else that was contrary and repugnant to the doctrine of the Roman church. While some of them exclaimed: '*blasphemavit*', others got up to leave, but they could do nothing more because of the king's presence.

Once silence had been restored, de Bèze said: '*Messieurs*, I beg you to wait for the end which will satisfy you.' He resumed his argument and followed it through. Then, having concluded his speech, he presented the Confession of the reformed churches to the king, who received it graciously from the *sieur* de la Ferté, captain of the guard, before handing it over to the prelates.

The Cardinal of Tournon then rose and spoke so quietly that he was barely audible. In brief, he begged the king not to believe what he had heard and to remain loyal to the faith of his forebears since King Clovis, in which he had been and would continue to be nurtured by the queen his mother, and he prayed to the glorious Virgin Mary and all the saints to assist him in this. He also asked for a chance to reply to the speech, adding that he would give a good answer. The king, he said, after hearing it, would be won back, but he suddenly corrected himself: 'not won back', he said, 'but continue to follow the right path'. He spoke these words very angrily and as though much distraught.

The queen replied that nothing had been done except by the decision of the council and on the advice of the *Parlement* of Paris; the intention was not to innovate or bring about change, but to quell the troubles caused by divergent religious views and to indicate the right path to those who had strayed from it.

Baum and Cunitz, [2], vol. 1, pp. 503–21.

DOCUMENT 4   MONLUC IN GUYENNE, 1562

The military career of Blaise de Monluc (c. 1501–77) spanned the Italian Wars and the French Wars of Religion. He first achieved fame by defending Siena in 1554, but he is remembered mainly on account of his lively memoirs, called Commentaires, *which he wrote in old age partly to vindicate his reputation. During the religious wars, he fought the Huguenots, often with great cruelty. He believed that 'one man hanged is worth a hundred killed in battle'. In 1562 he was sent to Guyenne to restore order. He was accompanied by two judges, Compain and Girard, but their concern for legal forms exasperated him.*

At Villefranche we met the Cardinal of Armagnac, who was waiting for us with a complaint that some of his churches had been destroyed, even at

Villefranche within the diocese of Rodez. When the consuls realised that we were approaching, they arrested four or five of the chief troublemakers, whom we found imprisoned. On the day we arrived the aforesaid *sieurs* d'Alesme and de Ferron came, but the commissioners would not accept them as they had not got letters patent from the king. In the end, however, we accepted them ... They began to try the four or five men who had been arrested by the Cardinal d'Armagnac, but Compain and Girard could not be persuaded to pass judgement, although they were given proof by the leading townsmen of countless rapes and thefts in addition to the destruction of the churches. They sat on the case for eight or ten days before deciding that the prisoners should be released. Although Monsieur de Ferron was of their religion, he concluded, like Monsieur d'Alesmes, that they should be executed. The Cardinal of Armagnac and all the officers despaired of justice being done and feared a calamity if justice were not done after our departure. Eventually d'Alesmes and de Ferron came to my lodging and said that one could not expect those men ever to pass sentence on their co-religionists and that they themselves wished to go as they would never achieve anything with them. I urged them to remain, whereupon d'Alesmes said: 'Do you wish to do something worthy of your name? Hang them from the windows of the town hall and that will settle the matter; otherwise justice will not be done.' I asked them if this was their shared opinion. 'Yes' was their reply and that was enough for me. Calling the sergeant of Monsieur de Saint-Orens, I said in their presence: 'Sergeant, fetch me the gaoler.' This he did and I said to the gaoler: 'Hand your prisoners over to him; and you, sergeant, fetch my two executioners, and hang the prisoners from the town hall windows.' He left immediately and within fifteen minutes we saw the prisoners dangling from the windows.

Blaise de Monluc, *Commentaires*, [15], vol. 2, pp. 435–7.

DOCUMENT 5   THE SITUATION IN 1562: A VENETIAN
            VIEW OF FRANCE

Montmorency and the Guises were so irritated by the Colloquy of Poissy that they left the court late in October 1561, followed by their supporters. Catherine de' Medici, finding herself drawn towards the Huguenots, caused the Edict of St Germain to be promulgated on 17 January 1562. It allowed them to worship publicly outside towns and privately within them. This is how the Venetian ambassador, Michieli, viewed the strength of the Huguenots.

There is no province that is not infected [with heresy] and there are some where the epidemic has spread even to the countryside, such as Normandy, almost the whole of Brittany, Touraine, Poitou, Guyenne, Gascony, a large part of Languedoc, Dauphiné, Provence, and Champagne, which amounts to nearly three-quarters of the kingdom. In countless places, the heretics hold meetings, called assemblies, in which they read, preach, live in the manner of Geneva without regard for the king's ministers or his commands. The epidemic has spread to all classes, and (oddly enough) to ecclesiastics, priests, monks, nuns and to almost entire convents, few of which are free of this plague. The disease is not always visible externally: persecution has kept it in order and so far it has erupted only among the populace who have virtually nothing to lose save their lives. Those who are afraid of losing both their lives and property simultaneously show less haste, but Your Serenity should believe that except for the lowest sort of people, those who attend church most devoutly and stay loyal to the Catholic faith, the rest are all considered to be deeply infected. The nobles especially are contaminated, notably those below the age of forty. Several still attend mass and observe the Catholic ceremonies, but they do so out of fear; if they think no one is watching them, they give up the mass above all and avoid the churches as far as possible. When it became clear that imprisonment, penalties and burnings made things worse, it was decided to prosecute only those who went around preaching, seducing the masses and holding public assemblies, and to leave the rest alone. The prisons in Paris and other towns of the kingdom were emptied: a very large number of people were set free, who have remained in the kingdom and are now preaching in public. They speak boldly and boast of having defeated the Papists, which is the name they give to their enemies. Thus all fear of persecution has gone: a kind of truce has been tacitly granted. Previously, as soon as they fell under suspicion, they fled to Germany or England, but mostly to Geneva. Since then, not only have they stopped going, but those who had gone into exile have returned. On my way to Italy I passed through Geneva and was told that after the death of the late king [Francis II] many nobles, who had retired there after the Tumult of Amboise, had gone back to France. They were followed by fifty of those they call ministers, responding to calls from several parts of France to preach the Word (which is what they call the Gospel as taught in accordance with their doctrine).

N. Tommaseo, [20], vol. 1, pp. 412–15.

DOCUMENT 6   PROMISES TO AVENGE THE MURDER OF FRANCIS, DUKE OF GUISE, 1563

Supporters of the Catholic family of Guise blamed the Huguenot leader, Admiral Coligny, for the murder of Francis, duke of Guise, in February 1563. They were also angered by the Peace of Amboise which conceded limited rights of worship to the Huguenots. So they decided to take the law into their own hands and exact retribution. Here are two terrifying oaths sworn by clients of the Guises, which reflect their hatred of the Huguenots and even of Catherine de' Medici's government.

1. I the undersigned promise and swear by the living God to keep and maintain the association made with the captains, lords and knights of the order to avenge the death of Monsieur the Duke of Guise, rendering service and fidelity to Messieurs his brothers, Madame his wife and Monsieur his son, as I had promised to the said late Duke of Guise, whom God absolve, for the recovery of the rights he had claimed without exception or reserve. I promise also to use all my strength up to my last breath to expel from this kingdom or to kill those who have made peace without punishing the murder, and to inflict a shameful death on those who shared in the homicide, and I swear also to use all my strength in exterminating those of the new religion. In order to carry out the above, I promise to stand by to march on 27 October with my associates and those in my charge and to go wherever Monsieur de Monluc shall direct me to go for the accomplishment of the association. And as a guarantee of the strict fulfilment of the above promises, I sign these presents with my hand and seal them with my seal. 2 August 1563. Signed: Sansac, and sealed.

2. I the undersigned promise and swear by the living God to render such obedience and loyal service to the Duke of Guise, the cardinals his uncles, and to his mother, as I had promised to the late Duke of Guise, for the recovery of his property as to avenge the death of the said Duke up to the fourth generation of those who committed the said homicide or connived at it and of those who are yet defending the culprits. To this effect I am ready to march with my associates and company on 27 September next, promising to obey the orders of Monsieur de Monluc whom I recognize as lieutenant-general of the enterprise in Guyenne. And as a guarantee of the above I sign these presents with my hand and seal them with my arms, 16 August 1563. Signed: Guy de Daillon, and sealed.

Chantilly: Musée Condé. Papiers de Condé, [1], Série L, vol. xix, f.59.

DOCUMENT 7   THE HUGUENOT STATE IN THE SOUTH, 1572

The following extracts are from a document containing forty clauses originally published in the Réveille-Matin des Français, *an anonymous pamphlet of 1574. It cannot be ascribed to any particular Huguenot assembly, but it throws an interesting light on the state of mind of the Huguenots of the Midi following the massacre of St Bartholomew. It may have influenced the decisions taken by their assemblies in 1573, which effectively set up an autonomous republican state in the south of France.*

1. Until such time as it may please God (who rules the hearts of kings) to change that of the king and restore the state of France to good order or to

arrange for a neighbouring prince of proven virtue to liberate this poor afflicted people: they will, after swearing an oath, elect by a public vote in their town or city a leader or 'major', who shall command the army for their defence and run the civil administration.

2. For each of the said majors they will elect a council of twenty-four men, who, like the major, will be chosen without regard to status from among the nobles or commoners of the town or surrounding countryside who are known for their public spirit.

3. In addition to the twenty-four and the major, making twenty-five in all, another seventy-five men will be elected so as to bring the total up to one hundred. These will be chosen likewise from the inhabitants of the town and neighbouring countryside. Their jurisdiction will apply to criminal cases only, that is to say offences punishable by death, banishment or mutilation.

4. The major will take no decision or action in military or civil matters without first consulting the twenty-four. Nor will the twenty-five be allowed to decide anything of public importance, such as a new law, the cancellation of a fiscal law, the levy of taxes or the signing of a truce or peace treaty, without the assent of the hundred.

6. On 1 January each year the twenty-five will resign their charges in the assembly of a hundred and revert to being private persons (albeit as members of the hundred). On their advice new elections will take place of a major and twenty-four councillors in the manner described above, excluding those who had just resigned ... The major will not be eligible for re-election for two years at least, but he will remain a member of the twenty-four for one year; only twenty-three, therefore, will need to be elected and the new major, who will be the twenty-fifth.

11. The leaders and councils will elect a commander-in-chief [*chef général*] in the manner of a Roman dictator who will command in the countryside and whom the inhabitants of the towns and cities will obey ...

12. Although it is not always possible in wartime to obtain advice, a council will be elected in the same way whose advice the commander-in-chief will seek whenever the occasion arises and necessity allows.

13. To obviate the calumnies which are often spread against the leaders and chief members of the state by enemy cunning, ambition or similar evils which Satan often introduces into the church, or which spring from certain suspicions easily stirred up among the soldiers or the people, and also to avoid the disturbances that are often caused by them, each townsman will be entitled to bring before the major and his council accusations against any noblemen or others whom they suspect of plotting against the public interest ...

35. When negotiating the leaders should bear in mind the following rules: never trust those who have so often and so treacherously broken faith and the public peace; never disarm as long as the enemy continues to oppose the true faith and those who profess it; and sign no peace treaties that can be used to start massacres. Before reaching an agreement the leaders should ensure first that it will be to the glory of God; secondly that it will

guarantee the safety of the poor churches, so that they will never again be left to the mercy of wolves and tigers.

Haag, [8], vol. x, pp. 104–9.

DOCUMENT 8   *FRANCOGALLIA* BY FRANÇOIS HOTMAN, 1573

Francogallia is one of the most famous political texts thrown up by the Huguenot party during the French Wars of Religion. It was published in 1573, and has often been seen as a reply to the massacre of St Bartholomew. In fact, much of the book was written before 1568 and formed part of a revival of Huguenot constitutional thought coinciding with the second civil war. On the surface, Francogallia *is a work of antiquarianism: it deals with Gauls, Romans and Franks. Its real purpose, however, was to legitimise Huguenot resistance to the Crown. In Hotman's view, the highest administrative authority in the kingdom was vested in the Estates-General, not the monarchy.*

I think it is abundantly clear from these references and from many other similar ones that the kings of Francogallia were constituted by the authoritative decision and desire of the people, that is, of the orders, or, as we are now accustomed to say, of the estates, rather than by any hereditary right. The custom employed by our ancestors in the installation of kings is another powerful argument to the same effect. We may observe that the custom we have remarked a little earlier, which Cornelius Tacitus reported of the Caninefates, the fellow-countrymen of the Franks – namely, the placing of the designated king upon a shield and his elevation upon the shoulders of those present – this was the custom practised among our kings. For he who had been chosen by the votes of the people was placed upon a shield, lifted up, and borne three times round the assembly of the electors, or, if the ceremony occurred in a military camp, round the ranks of the army amid general applause and acclamation ...

It is to be understood that, in as much as it was the right and power of the estates and the people to constitute and maintain kings, so, if at least all our annals do not lie, the supreme power of deposing kings was also that of the people. The very first man to be made king of Francogallia offers us a remarkable proof of his power. When the people discovered that he was given to shameful acts and libidinous behaviour, spending his time in debauchery and fornication, they removed him by public consent and expelled him from Gaul. Our annals show this to have happened in the year 469.

F. Hotman, *Francogallia*, [10], pp. 231–3; p. 235.

DOCUMENT 9   *THE RIGHT OF MAGISTRATES* BY
              THÉODORE DE BÈZE, 1574

Of all the sixteenth-century political treatises Du droit des magistrats *was
one of the most original and influential. It expounded clearly and
persuasively the theory justifying armed resistance by the Huguenots to the
French Crown. The author, Théodore de Bèze, was Calvin's lieutenant in
Geneva. After the latter's death in 1564 he assumed the leadership of the
Calvinist movement. He wrote* Du droit des magistrats *in June and July
1573, following a period of intense political activity. It was first published
anonymously in Heidelberg in 1574. The almost contemporary historian,
J.A. de Thou, blamed it in part for the renewal of civil war in that year.*

I come now to the lesser magistrates who hold a lower rank between the
sovereign and the people. I do not mean officers of the king's household,
but those who have public or state responsibilities either in the
administration of justice or in war. In a monarchy, therefore, the latter are
called 'officers of the crown' and thus of the kingdom rather than the king,
which are two quite different things ...

Now, although all these officers are beneath their sovereign in that they
take commands from him and are installed in office and approved by him,
they hold, properly speaking, not of the sovereign but of the sovereignty.
That is why, when the sovereign magistrate dies, they nonetheless remain in
office, just as the sovereignty itself remains intact ...

It is thus apparent that there is a mutual obligation between the king and
the officers of a kingdom; that the government of the kingdom is not in the
hands of the king in its entirety but only the sovereign degree; that each of
the officers has a share in accord with his degree; and that there are definite
conditions on either side. If these conditions are not observed by the inferior
officers, it is the part of the sovereign to dismiss and punish them, but only
for definite cause and according to the procedures prescribed by the law of
the realm, and not otherwise, unless he is himself to violate the oath he took
to exercise his office in conformity with law. If the king, hereditary or
elective, clearly goes back on the conditions without which he would not
have been recognized and acknowledged, can there be any doubt that the
lesser magistrates of the kingdom, of the cities, and of the provinces, the
administration of which they have received from the sovereignty itself, are
free of their oath, at least to the extent that they are entitled to resist
flagrant oppression of the realm which they swore to defend and protect
according to their office and particular jurisdiction?

What, it will be asked? Is a ruler, previously regarded as sovereign and
inviolable, suddenly to be considered a private person at the whim of some
subordinate, and then pursued and attacked as if a public enemy? Not at
all, I say, for this would open the door to all kinds of miserable seditions
and conspiracies. I am speaking, in the first place, of a clearly flagrant
tyranny and of a tyrant who endures no remonstrations. Furthermore, I do

not speak of removing a tyrant from his throne, but only of resistance against open violence according to one's rank. For I have already shown that an obligation entered into by common agreement cannot be nullified at the discretion of any individual, no matter who he is and no matter how just his complaint.

On the other hand, it is by the sovereignty itself that lesser officers are charged with enforcing and maintaining law among those committed to their charge, to which duty they are further bound by oath. (And they are not absolved from this oath by the delinquency of a king who has turned tyrant and flagrantly violated the conditions to which he swore and under which he was received as king.) Is it not then reasonable, by all law divine and human, that more should be permitted to these lesser magistrates, in view of their sworn duty to preserve the law, than to purely private persons without office? I say, therefore, that they are obliged, if reduced to that necessity, and by force of arms where that is possible, to offer resistance to flagrant tyranny, and to safeguard those within their care, until such time as the Estates, or whoever holds the legislative power of the kingdom or the empire, may by common deliberation make further and appropriate provision for the public welfare. This, moreover, is not to be seditious or disloyal towards one's sovereign, but to be loyal fully and to keep one's faith toward those from whom one's office was received against him who has broken his oath and oppressed the kingdom he ought to have protected.

J.H. Franklin, [7], pp. 110–12.

DOCUMENT 10   THE PEACE OF MONSIEUR, 6 MAY 1576

The Edict of Beaulieu, confirming the Peace of Monsieur, consisted of sixty-three clauses, of which only the more important are cited here. As well as providing protection for the Catholic church, it made important concessions to the Huguenots, including the famous chambres mi-parties *in the* parlements. *It represented the most favourable settlement so far achieved by the Huguenots, but the extreme Catholics, led by the Guises, found it wholly unacceptable.*

4.   In order to remove any cause of dissension from among our subjects, we hereby permit the free, public and general exercise of the Protestant faith [*religion prétendue réformée*] in all the towns and localities of our kingdom ... without restriction of time or person ... and in these towns and localities Protestants will be allowed to preach, pray, sing psalms, administer baptism and the Last Supper, celebrate marriages, have schools and do anything else pertaining to the free and complete exercise of their faith. They may hold consistories and synods, both provincial and national, and summon our officers to those places where the said synods will meet, and we hereby enjoin our officers, or some of them, to attend the said assemblies. But we command all Protestants to abstain from the practice of their religion in our

city of Paris and its suburbs within a radius of two leagues from it, but no action will be taken against Protestants who worship in their own homes; nor will their children or their tutors be forced to do anything that contradicts or prejudices their faith. Protestants are also forbidden to practise their faith in our court and within two leagues from it, as also in our territories beyond the Alps, reserving their right to worship within their homes. Our wish and chief purpose is to reunite our subjects within a single religion, and we hope that God will gradually bring this about by means of a free and holy general council.

18. Since the administration of justice is one of the chief means of maintaining peace among our subjects, and in response to a demand from our united Catholic[1] and Protestant subjects, we hereby order the creation in our *Parlement* of Paris of a chamber comprising two presidents and sixteen councillors, half of them Catholic and half Protestant. These officers, whom we shall appoint ourselves, will receive the same wages, honours, powers and prerogatives as other councillors of the said court. And we shall send the said court to our town of Poitiers for three months in each year from 1 June till 31 October to dispense justice to our united Catholic and Protestant subjects in Poitou, Angoumois, Aunis and La Rochelle ...

19. For the area covered by the jurisdiction of the *Parlement* of Toulouse a chamber will be set up at Montpellier comprising two presidents and eighteen councillors, half of them Catholic and half Protestant.

20. Similar chambers will be set up in our *parlements* of Grenoble, Bordeaux, Aix, Dijon, Rouen and Brittany, each with two presidents and ten councillors, half of them Catholic and half Protestant.

23. We command our beloved brother-in-law, the king of Navarre, our beloved cousin the Prince of Condé, our beloved cousin the lord of Damville, Marshal of France, and similarly all other noblemen of whatever quality and degree, both united Catholic and Protestant, to be restored to such governorships, charges, estates and royal offices as they held before 24 August 1572, without requiring new letters of appointment and regardless of any judgments given against them in the past or of any letters of appointment others may have received in respect of the same offices. Likewise they will recover all their property, rights, titles etc., notwithstanding any sentences passed as a result of the recent disturbances which are hereby declared null and void.

34. Having already declared null and void the judgments pronounced against the late lord of Châtillon, Admiral of France, we now order them to be erased from the registers of our *Parlements* and other courts, and the lands of the said Admiral to remain in the possession of his children, notwithstanding the decrees which had annexed them to the royal domain.

36. We forbid any procession to commemorate the death of our late

---

[1] The *catholiques associés* or *unis* were the party of Henri de Montmorency-Damville.

cousin, the Prince of Condé, or St Bartholomew's day, as well as any other action likely to revive memories of the troubles.

59. As soon as this decree has been published the united Catholics and Protestants will remove all their garrisons from the towns, fortresses, châteaux and houses belonging to us or to private persons, including the clergy, and restore them to the peaceful condition they enjoyed before the past and current troubles. However, for certain good reasons we have entrusted to the care of the said united Catholics and Protestants the following eight towns: Aiguesmortes and Beaucaire in Languedoc, Périgueux and le Mas-de-Verdun in Guyenne, Nyons and Serres (the town and the château) in Dauphiné, Issoire in Auvergne and Seine la Grand' Tour (and its circumference) in Provence. Our said brother, the king of Navarre, the Prince of Condé, Marshal Damville and those to whom the said towns have been committed for safekeeping will swear on their faith and honour to carry out this task well and loyally. We promise for our part not to impose any governor or garrison on any other town held or to be restored by them, other than existed of old and in the reign of our late father, King Henry. Similarly, in order to bring as much relief as possible to our subjects in all our other towns, we promise that they will get no garrison or governor other than existed in our father's reign. Nor do we want any châteaux, towns, houses or property belonging to private persons of any degree to have garrisons other than those normally based there in peace time.

Haag, [8], *Pièces justificatives*, pp. 127–41.

DOCUMENT 11   THE ROYAL *MIGNONS*, JULY 1576

The encouragement given by Henry III to the duels and scandals of his favourites or mignons *did serious harm to his reputation among the Parisians. They were also shocked by the fiscal expedients he devised to extract money from the official classes in the capital. In 1575 there were riots led by some officers of the urban militia against the king's Italian tax-farmers. The mood of the capital is reflected in the following extract from the diary of Pierre de l'Estoile (1546–1611), a Parisian lawyer.*

It was at this time that the *mignons* began to be much talked about by the common people, who hated them not only because of their foolish and haughty ways and of their effeminate and immodest make-up and clothes, but above all on account of the huge gifts heaped upon them by the king. The people blamed them for their impoverishment, though actually the *mignons* did not keep money for long; it reverted to the people almost as surely as water pours from a drain-pipe. These pretty *mignons* had their hair pomaded, curled and recurled and tied over small velvet bonnets in the manner of prostitutes. Their shirt collars were so stiff and wide that their heads looked like that of St John on the platter ... Their favourite pastimes were gambling, blaspheming, leaping, dancing, pirouetting, quarrelling and wenching. They followed the king everywhere and in any company, seeking only to please him by word and deed. They feared and honoured him more than God and their sole concern was to keep his favour.

L'Estoile, [12], p. 122.

DOCUMENT 12   *THE DEFENCE OF LIBERTY AGAINST TYRANTS* BY PHILIPPE DU PLESSIS-MORNAY, 1579

The authorship of the Vindiciae contra tyrannos *(The Defence of Liberty against Tyrants) has been disputed, but it is most often ascribed to Philippe Du Plessis-Mornay (1549–1623), a Huguenot nobleman who became one of the most trusted advisers of King Henry IV. The* Vindiciae *is one of a trilogy of highly influential Huguenot political texts seeking to justify armed resistance to the Valois monarchy. Among its distinctive features is the theory of the state originating in a twofold contract between God and the king, and God and the people.*

When kings were given to the people, this compact did not lapse but was instead confirmed and constantly renewed. We have said that at the coronation of a king a twofold covenant was made. The first was between God, the king, and the people. (Indeed, the people are put first in *Chronicles* 2: 23.) And its purpose was that the people should become God's people, that is that they should be God's Church. Why God covenanted with the king we have already shown: why, with the whole people we must now inquire. For it is certain that God did not require this in vain. And it would have been an empty covenant if there were not some authority remaining in the people to make a promise and to keep it. It seems, therefore, that God did what auditors so often do with borrowers of doubtful credit, which is to obligate several for the same amount so that there are two or more co-signers for the single loan, each one of whom may be held responsible for the entire sum as though he were the principal debtor. Since it was dangerous to entrust the Church to a single, all-too-human individual, the Church was committed and entrusted to the people as a whole. The king, situated on a slippery height, could easily have fallen into irreligion. Hence, God wished to have the people intervene, so that the Church might not be ruined with the king ...

It is, furthermore, the part of a good legislator not only to make sure that delinquencies are punished, but to prevent them from being committed, just as good physicians would rather prescribe diets to prevent disease than remedies for the symptoms. Hence, a religious people not only will restrain a prince in the act of doing violence to God's Law, but will, from the beginning, prevent gradual changes arising from his guilt or negligence, for the true worship of God may be slowly corrupted over extended periods of time. Moreover, they will not only refuse to tolerate crimes committed against God's majesty in public, but will constantly strive to remove all occasions for such crimes. We, thus, read that King Hezekiah, with Israel convened in public assembly, warned those who lived beyond the Jordan to smash the bronze serpent they had made and also the altar they had built for it.

It is, then, not only lawful for Israel to resist a king who overturns the Law and the Church of God, but if they do not do so they are guilty of the same crime and are subject to the same penalty. Hence, if they are attacked with words, they will resist with words, but if with force, with force, and with stratagems, I say, as well as open warfare ...

When we speak of the people collectively, we mean those who receive authority from the people, that is, the magistrates below the king who have been elected by the people or established in some other way. These take the place of the people assembled as a whole and are ephors to kings and associates in their rule. And we also mean the assembly of the Estates, which are nothing less than the epitome of a kingdom to which all public matters are referred.

J.H. Franklin, [7], pp. 146–9.

DOCUMENT 13   **THE DAY OF THE BARRICADES, 12 MAY 1588**

Early on Thursday 12 May the king ordered a company of Swiss troops and one of French soldiers of his guard to take up positions on the Petit Pont ... one of French soldiers on the Pont Saint-Michel, three of Swiss troops and one of French at the Place de Grève, four of Swiss and two of French in the cemetery of the Innocents, and the rest of the four thousand Swiss and the other French companies around the palace of the Louvre. The king thus hoped to give effect to a decision he and his council had taken long before to arrest a number of Parisian bourgeois, Leaguers, prominent people and followers of the duke of Guise (who, he claimed, had formed a faction and plotted to capture and depose him) and to execute them as an example to the duke's other followers, whom he had deceived by covering up his damnable and ambitious designs with the mask of religion. The king's plan was revealed that morning by President Séguier (somewhat rashly for such a high-ranking courtier) to a Leaguer who wanted to know the cause of the commotion. The chancellor explained that everyone ought to be master in his own house, and that the king would show his mettle that day by freeing those who had served him well and punishing the rebels and troublemakers. But the king's plan misfired, for the people, seeing his troops posted in different parts of the city, began to stir. They feared worse to come and complained that no foreign garrison had ever been seen or heard of in Paris before. Whereupon each took up arms and, taking to the streets, stretched chains across them and erected barricades at the cross-roads. Workmen left their tools, merchants their businesses, solicitors [*procureurs*] their bundles, and barristers their caps; even the presidents and councillors [of the *Parlement*] seized halberds. One could only hear dreadful shouts, murmurs and seditious words aimed at exciting or alarming the people. And just as a secret, love or wine becomes worthless once it has been exposed, so the duke of Guise, having discovered the king's secret (as the king had discovered his) and fearing that he might be forestalled, sent several noblemen secretly to each district so as to encourage the people, who, though rebellious, were cowardly, and to instruct them on how best to defend themselves with barricades ...

The king, who until midday was the stronger party and disposed of the means to foil the plans and destroy the barricades of the Guisards and the Parisians, sheathed his sword and forbade his men to draw theirs more than half-way on pain of death, hoping that moderation, sweetness and fair words would appease the fury of the rebels and gradually disarm the foolish populace. But the opposite happened: that afternoon the people, being armed and mobilised behind their barricades, felt strong, and began to defy the Swiss and French troops by looks and words, threatening to kill them unless they withdrew. Hearing about this, the king sent the Seigneur d'O, Captain Alphonse, Marshals Biron and d'Aumont, Grillon and many others to remove all the foreign and French troops as quietly as possible to the Louvre. But before this could be done, a fight developed near the Petit-Pont and the Marché Neuf, causing casualties among the Swiss. As the seigneurs d'O and Corse led them across the Pont Notre Dame, they begged the people to let them pass unharmed. But neither they nor the poor Swiss, who threw down their arms crying 'Good France!' and, wringing their hands, 'have mercy!', could check the mob's fury. From the Petit-Pont to the Pont Notre Dame many Swiss were killed by shots from arquebuses and other weapons or by rocks and stones hurled from the windows by women and children. Others, who surrendered shouting 'Long live Guise!', were disarmed by Monsieur de Brissac and held in the meat market of the Marché Neuf, while the dead were buried in the middle of the *parvis** Notre Dame. The rest of the king's guard crossed the bridge with much difficulty, and the seigneurs d'O and Corse, who led them, faced great personal danger. They admitted that they had never been so scared as on that occasion.

The troops stationed at the Grève and the Innocents were, like the rest, in danger of being cut to pieces. They were rescued, along with the wretched Swiss prisoners, by the duke of Guise. At the urgent request and prayer of the king, who had sent him Marshal Biron to that end, he went to fetch them and led them to safety. If it had not been for him they would all have perished. The Swiss have since acknowledged their debt to the duke, who asked the people to hand them over to him. The foolish populace complied immediately, for it was as easily appeased by the voice of the duke of Guise as it was poisoned and stupefied by his love. He had been in his lodging all day. Wearing a white slashed doublet and a large hat, he stood at the window of the Hôtel de Guise till four p.m., when he left to perform that service for the king. As he emerged, some louts, who had gathered to see him go by, shouted: 'Stop messing about! Take Monsieur [the Cardinal of Bourbon] to Rheims!' As the duke walked along the streets the people vied with each other as to who would shout 'Long live Guise!' the loudest. He pretended to dislike this and, doffing his large hat (no one knows if he was laughing behind it) he told them repeatedly: 'That's enough, my friends. That is too much, *Messieurs*. You must shout:"Long live the king!" ...'

L'Estoile, [12], pp. 551–4.

DOCUMENT 14   THE MURDER OF HENRY, THIRD DUKE
OF GUISE, AT BLOIS, 23 DECEMBER 1588

Some of the most graphic accounts of events in France during the Wars of Religion were written by Étienne Pasquier (1529–1615), a distinguished Parisian barrister. In the autumn of 1588 he and his friend, Montaigne, attended the Estates-General at Blois as spectators. Although he remained a Catholic all his life, Pasquier had Huguenot friends, and tried always to be scrupulously impartial in judging events. He was a politique *and hated war. Writing about the murder of Guise, he wondered if, all things considered, he would not have committed the same crime as Henry III had he been faced with the same challenge.*

To Monsieur Airault, *lieutenant criminel** of Angers.
   I am about to tell you of the most tragic event that has ever taken place in France. On 23 December Monsieur de Guise was murdered in the king's chamber, and next day it was the turn of his brother, the cardinal. You are already trembling, I am sure, but I am only telling you the truth. However, no more blood was shed, for the rest escaped, were imprisoned or pardoned.
   Let me give you a blow-by-blow account of what happened. The king, angered by various decisions taken against him in our assembly, blamed those two princes for them. The more concessions he made to the deputies, the more they demanded of him, rather like the hydra, who, having had one head cut off produces another seven. Three or four days earlier Monsieur de Guise had quarrelled with the king over the post of *Lieutenant-Général* and the town of Orléans. The king therefore decided to have the two princes murdered, believing that those demands would cease with their deaths.
   This is what he did. On 22nd of this month he informed Monsieur de

Guise of his plan to leave next day for La Noue [a country house situated half a league away from the château of Blois] and to stay there till Christmas eve. He said that, before leaving, he wanted all the members of his council [*conseil des finances*] to meet early in the morning to settle certain matters he would put before them. At the same time, he ordered ten or twelve noblemen from among his 'Forty-five' to accompany him, booted and spurred. He also held over certain petitions submitted by the seigneurs de Rieux and Alphonse Corse.

All these people turned up at the appointed time and place: Corse, Rieux and the secretaries of state met in the king's study and the rest in his chamber. The king, it is said, complained to the latter that he had been under the tutelage of the Guises for far too long and that the more he had obliged them, the more they had disobeyed him. If he had ten thousand reasons for being angry with them since they had rebelled, he had even more since the opening of the Estates. He had therefore decided to get rid of them, not by legal means (for Monsieur de Guise commanded so much support in this place that he would end up trying his own judges) but by murdering them in his chamber. The time had come, he continued, for him to be the only king, adding that whoever had a companion also had a master. After he had spoken thus, everyone present promised him their support. The seigneurs de Rieux and Corse and the secretaries of state, Beaulieu and Revolt, remained in the king's study; ten or twelve of the 'Forty-five' in his chamber, and Marshal d'Aumont and the seigneur de Larchant in the council chamber. Some people believe that these two had been taken into the king's secret, as the sequel was to prove.

Although this enterprise was planned as secretly as possible, some knowledge of it leaked out. As Monsieur de Guise left his room to attend the council, he met on the terrace of the château a nobleman from Auvergne, called La Sale, who warned him against proceeding any further because of a trap that had been laid for him. Thanking him, Guise said: 'my good friend, I have long been cured of that fear'. Four or five steps further on, he received a similar warning from a Picard, called Aubencour (unless I am mistaken), who had once been his servant. The duke called him a fool. But on entering the council chamber, he seemed to draw back, for he noticed at the door several guards belonging to the seigneur de Larchant, and then Marshal d'Aumont, who did not usually attend the council. He asked for an explanation and Larchant said that he had come to ask for the wages due to his soldiers whose quarter had just ended; but he could not say why d'Aumont was there.

Standing in front of the hearth, Guise dropped a handkerchief by chance or design and stepped on it. It was picked up by the seigneur de Fontenay, treasurer of the *Épargne*, and the duke asked him to take it to his secretary, Péricart, and to bring him another at once. Many people believe (but this is only an opinion) that the duke's action was to warn his friends of the danger in which he saw himself. As Péricart tried to enter the chamber his way was barred by the archers of the guard.

Meanwhile, the Cardinal of Guise and the archbishop of Lyons arrived. Everyone then sat down at the council table. Larchant complained that his archers had not been paid, and Marcel, the *intendant des finances*, pointed out that some money was available that would satisfy them in part. Monsieur de Guise complained of feeling unwell, whereupon St Prix, the king's *valet de chambre**, brought him the king's box of plums. Soon afterwards, the secretary of state, Nervol [i.e. Revol], entered, saying that the king wished to see the duke. Guise rose to his feet and, twirling his cloak this way and that, as if in jest, entered the king's chamber, its door being closed immediately behind him. He found himself surrounded by a dozen noblemen who had been waiting for him in silence. They greeted him with many blows of such violence that he merely groaned.

This could not be done quietly. The cardinal and the archbishop, suspecting the truth, tried to rush in, but were stopped by Marshal d'Aumont, who, putting his hand upon his sword as an officer of the Crown, forbade anyone to move on pain of death. Thereafter the *sieur* de Richelieu, the *Grand prévôt*, went to the hall of the Third Estate and arrested the president de Nuilly, de Marteau, *prévôt des marchands** [i.e. the Mayor of Paris], Compan, Cotteblanche, aldermen [*échevins*] of Paris and others. He told them that they were to sit in judgement on two soldiers who had tried to kill the king. At the same time the Cardinal of Guise, the archbishop of Lyons and, soon afterwards, the Cardinal of Bourbon, *messieurs* de Nemours, d'Elboeuf and the Prince of Joinville were taken prisoner. The same fate befell *mesdames* de Nemours and d'Aumale, though the latter was released next day ...

There was much alarm in town: all the shops were shut, and it rained heavily all day, as if to warn us of the calamities in store ... That same day the Cardinal of Guise was stabbed to death in his cell by four soldiers of Captain Gast, and the bodies of the two brothers were burnt on the following night, for the king was afraid that if they were buried their bones would be taken as relics by the Parisians (which seems likely). As for the archbishop of Lyons, his life was spared by the intercession of his nephew, the Baron de Luz ... The king wanted to hang Nuilly, Marteau and Compan, but he was dissuaded by Monsieur de Ris, first president of [the *parlement* of] Brittany ... That same day Monsieur Marcel was sent to placate the Parisians, as it was believed that he had gained their trust in the past. May it please God to spare him the fate that befell another Marcel in the days of Charles VI!

We are now waiting like a bird on a branch for news. Four days have passed since this tragedy took place and not a word has come from Paris, which makes me fear the worst for our interests. Farewell. From Blois, 27 December 1588.

E. Pasquier, [18], pp. 351–6.

DOCUMENT 15   THE ASSASSINATION OF HENRY III,
1 AUGUST 1589

On Tuesday 1 August a Dominican friar, called Jacques Clément, who was
between twenty-three and twenty-four years old and a native of Sorbonne, a
village four leagues away from Sens in Burgundy ... was admitted to the
king's presence in the house of Gondi at Saint-Cloud, thanks to Monsieur
de La Guesle, *procureur général* to the *Parlement* of Paris. It was about 8
a.m. when the king, sitting naked on his close stool except for a dressing
gown over his shoulders, was informed that a monk from Paris wished to
speak to him. Hearing that his guards were barring the monk's way, he
angrily ordered the monk to be admitted, saying that otherwise he would be
accused in Paris of chasing monks away. The Jacobin, with a knife hidden
up his sleeve, entered and introduced himself to the king, who, having just
risen, had not yet fastened his breeches. After making a deep bow, the
monk handed to the king a letter from the count of Brienne (who was then
a prisoner in Paris) and said that he had also been charged to convey an
important secret to him. The king, believing that he was in no danger from
such a weedy little monk, ordered his attendants to withdraw. He opened
the letter and began reading it, whereupon the monk, seeing the king thus
engrossed, pulled out his knife and plunged it deeply into the king's
abdomen just above the navel. With a great effort the king pulled it out and
struck the monk's left eyebrow with its point. At the same time he shouted:
'Ah! the wicked monk has killed me! Kill him!' The king's guards and
others, hearing his shouts, rushed into the room, and those nearest the
Jacobin felled him to the ground at the king's feet ... Afterwards the king,
having been put to bed, sent for the king of Navarre, who had gone to the
war, and ordered that all members of his entourage should be allowed to
enter his room. About seventy or eighty noblemen entered, fully armed, and
each of them in turn kissed the monarch's hand, which he held out most
graciously. That night, His Majesty, seeing that his life was ebbing away,
asked for mass to be said in his chamber and took communion. He then
spoke for some time to the king of Navarre, and, showing him to the
assembled nobles, declared: 'There is your king!'

L'Estoile, [12], pp. 643–5.

DOCUMENT 16   AN APOLOGIA FOR THE SIXTEEN, 1593

The Dialogue d'entre le Maheustre et le Manant *[Dialogue between the*
Courtier and the Labourer] is one of the last great polemical pamphlets of
the Catholic League. It was published anonymously in December 1593 and
was probably written by François Morin, sieur de Cromé, who became an
active member of the Sixteen after Henry III's assassination. He argues that

the Sixteen and their supporters were the only Leaguers who acted in accordance with their principles and religious convictions. They were betrayed by the aristocratic leaders of the League, who used the Sixteen for their own ends.

Maheustre: 'Whatever the Sixteen may do, all their plans and undertakings will be changed and corrupted, and to this end division will be sown in your party so that everything will be destroyed and lost. They would do much better to draw back from their actions and strive for peace and agreement with the king, as others are doing. If they do this, all the slanders that have been spread about them will cease; they will be loved and respected, and, instead of suffering hardships, torment, affliction and injuries, they will enjoy repose and tranquillity as well as honours and riches. If, on the other hand, they persist in their opinions and resistance, they will continue to be harassed and reviled, and will be destroyed along with the League.'

Manant: 'I know that you and your friends share that aim. But I also know that the Sixteen are good Catholics and will never recognise your heretical king, whatever obstacle, malice, hypocrisy and stratagem may be used by the great nobles [*les grands*] of this world, who have spoilt everything by conniving and intriguing with your party. If only they had been as resolute as the Sixteen, your party would have been destroyed long ago; but the *grands* have ruined everything and have gone directly against the interests of the Catholic party. When members of the *Parlement* were imprisoned, along with several leaders of the nobility, the *grands* who led us pressed for their release and even offered themselves as sureties for them. Your party was very small and would not have doubled in size if those prisoners had not been freed ... Only the power of God has sustained the poor Catholics, who have been betrayed by most of their magistrates, royal office-holders and great families, and badly served by the governors and noblemen who led the party. Instead of making war on the heretics, they have come to terms with them and have helped each other at the expense of the people, falling on them like dogs. They have ruined the people utterly by levying tax upon tax for the benefit of the party leaders. They have exploited the blood and sweat of the poor, who have had to pay four times more for a piece of bread after it had passed through the hands of these aristocratic leeches. They have made a pact with the great families to ruin the preachers and the Sixteen on the pretext that they will not recognise the king of Navarre.'

Maheustre: 'I am pleased to hear you admit that the efforts and activities of the Sixteen have gone up in smoke. This shows that they should not be followed and that they ruin everything by stubbornly opposing the wishes of the *grands*. And do you find it so strange that our party should have been treated with courtesy? I assure you that we have returned it two-fold to those who have sought it from us and have not been ungracious to those who have asked for it. But your preachers and the Sixteen have forsaken our favours by opposing us so obstinately. As long as they persist in their

attitude, they will continue to be harassed, insulted, despised and hounded
to death, for they alone stand in the way of the king being recognised and
the war being brought to an end.'

Manant: 'The preachers, the Sixteen and the good Catholic people would
rather die as poor Catholics than as rich heretics; no injury, slander, outrage
or death threat will make them depart from their resolve never to recognise
the king of Navarre.'

Maheustre: 'It is unreasonable that those who want peace should suffer
because of the stubborn.'

Manant: 'It is even less reasonable to lose one's faith by recognising a
heretic.'

Cromé, [5], pp. 123–5.

DOCUMENT 17   THE EDICT OF NANTES, 13 APRIL 1598

*Although based on earlier peace settlements with the Huguenots, the Edict
of Nantes was far more detailed. It consisted of four documents: ninety-two
general articles, fifty-six secret articles and two royal warrants. The
following are among the more important clauses.*

GENERAL ARTICLES:

1. That the memory of all things passed on the one part or the other since
the beginning of March 1585 until our coming to the Crown, and also
during the other preceding troubles, and the occasion of the same, shall
remain extinguished and suppressed, as things that had never been ...
2. We prohibit all our subjects of whatever state and condition they be, to
renew the memory thereof, to attack, resent, injure, or provoke one another
by reproaches for what is past, under any pretext or cause whatsoever, by
disputing, contesting, quarrelling, reviling, or offending by factious words;
but to contain themselves, and live peaceably together as brethren, friends,
and fellow-citizens, upon penalty for acting to the contrary, to be punished
for breakers of peace, and disturbers of the public quiet.
3. We ordain that the Catholic religion shall be restored and reestablished
in all places and quarters of this kingdom and country under our obedience,
and where the exercise of the same faith has been intermitted, to be there
again, peaceably and freely exercised without any trouble or impediment ...
6. And not to leave any occasion of trouble and difference among our
subjects, we ... permit those of the Reformed Religion to live and dwell in
all the cities and places of this our kingdom and country under our
obedience, without being inquired after, vexed, molested, or compelled to
do any thing in religion contrary to their conscience, nor by reason of the

same be searched after in houses or places where they live, they comporting themselves in other things as is contained in this our present edict or statute.

9.   We permit also to those of the said religion to hold, and continue its exercise in all the cities and places under our obedience, where it has by them been established and made public by many and divers times, in 1586, and in 1597, until the end of August, notwithstanding all decrees and judgments whatsoever to the contrary.

14.   [They will not] exercise the said religion in our Court, nor in our territories and countries beyond the mountains, nor in our City of Paris, nor within five leagues of the said city: nevertheless those of the said religion dwelling in the said lands and countries beyond the mountains, and in our said city, and within five leagues about the same, shall not be searched after in their houses, nor constrained to do any thing in religion against their consciences, comporting themselves in all other things according as is contained in our present edict or law.

16.   Following the second Article of the Conference of Nérac, we grant to those of the said religion power to build places for its exercise in cities and places where it is granted them, and that those shall be rendered to them which they have heretofore built ...

20.   They shall also be obliged to keep and observe the festivals of the Catholic church, and shall not on the same days work, sell, or keep open shop, and likewise the artisans shall not work out of their shops, in their chambers or houses privately on the said festivals, and other forbidden days, of any trade, the noise whereof may be heard without by those that pass by, or by the neighbours.

21.   Books concerning the said reformed religion shall not be printed or sold publicly, save in the cities and places where its public exercise is permitted ...

22.   We ordain, that there shall not be made any difference or distinction on account of the said religion in receiving scholars to be instructed in the universities, colleges, or schools, or of the sick and poor into hospitals, sick houses or public almshouses.

25.   We will and ordain that all those of the reformed religion shall be obliged ... to pay tithes to the curates and other ecclesiastics and to all others to whom they shall appertain ...

27.   In order to re-unite so much better the minds and good will of our subjects ..., and to take away all complaints for the future; we declare all those ... of the said reformed religion to be capable of holding and exercising all estates, dignities, offices and public charges whatsoever ...

30.   So that justice may be given and administered to our subjects without any suspicion, hatred or favour, as being one of the principal means for the maintaining peace and concord, we ordain, that in our *parlement* of Paris shall be established a chamber, composed of a president and sixteen councillors of the said *parlement*, which shall be called ... the Chamber of the Edict, and it shall take cognisance not only of the causes and process of those of the said reformed religion which shall be within the jurisdiction of

the said court, but also of the appeals of our *parlements* of Normandy and Brittany ...

31. Besides the chamber heretofore established at Castres for appeals from our *parlement* of Toulouse, which shall remain as it is, we have for the same reasons ordained, and do ordain, that in each of our *parlements* of Grenoble and Bordeaux there shall be in like manner established a chamber, composed of two presidents, one Catholic, the other of the reformed religion, and twelve councillors, whereof six will be Catholics and the other six of the said religion ...

58. We declare all sentences, judgments, procedures, seizures, sales and decrees made and given against those of the reformed religion, as well living as dead, from the death of the deceased King Henry II ... upon the occasion of the said Religion, tumults and troubles since happening, as also the execution of the same judgments and decrees, henceforth cancelled, revoked and annulled.

82. All those of the said religion shall depart and desist henceforth from all practices, negotiations, and intelligences, as well within as without our kingdom; and the said assemblies and councils established within the provinces shall readily disband, and also all the leagues and associations made or to be made under what pretext soever, to the prejudice of the present edict, shall be cancelled and annulled ... prohibiting most expressly all our subjects to make henceforth any assessments or levies of money, fortifications, musters, congregations and assemblies other than such as are permitted by our present edict, and without arms ...

SECRET ARTICLES:

6. Concerning the article which mentions *bailliages*, the following declarations and concessions have been made. first, in order to establish the practice of the reformed religion in the two places granted in each *bailliage*, *sénéchaussée** and *gouvernement*, those of the reformed religion shall name two towns, in the suburbs of which the said worship shall be established by the commissioners His Majesty deputes to carry out the edict. And if these proposals are not approved by the commissioners, those of the said religion shall suggest two or three neighbouring townships or villages for each town from which the commissioners will then choose one ... Secondly, in the *gouvernement* of Picardy there will be only two towns in whose suburbs those of the said religion will be able to worship ...

33. A place shall be provided for those of the reformed religion to serve the town, *prévôté* and *vicomté** of Paris at not more than five leagues' distance from that town, in which they can worship publicly.

34. In all those places in which public worship is allowed, the people may be summoned, even by the ringing of bells, and there shall be all the usual activities and functions necessary to the practice of this religion, or to the maintenance of discipline, such as the holding of consistories, colloquies and provincial and national synods with His Majesty's permission.

35. The ministers, elders and deacons of the said religion shall not be obliged to appear in a court of justice to give evidence, for matters revealed in their consistories, if these are censures, except in matters concerning the king's person or the preservation of his state.

ROYAL WARRANT (3 APRIL 1598):

This day, the third day of April 1598, the king being at Nantes and desirous of showing kindness to his subjects of the so-called reformed religion, and helping them to meet several heavy expenses they have to bear, has commanded ... that in future, beginning from the first day of the current month, there shall be placed in the hand of M. de Vierse, whom His Majesty has specially commissioned for this purpose, by each successive treasurer of his coffers, an order for the sum of 45,000 *écus* to be used for certain secret matters which concern them, and which His Majesty does not wish to be specified or revealed ...

ROYAL WARRANT (30 APRIL 1598)

His Majesty in addition to what is contained in the edict he has recently drawn up ... has granted and promised them that all the fortified places, towns, châteaux which they held up to the end of last August, in which there will be garrisons, shall ... remain in their hands under the authority and allegiance of His Majesty for the space of eight years, counting from the day the said edict is published ... For the upkeep of the garrisons to be stationed in these towns, His Majesty has apportioned a sum not to exceed 180,000 crowns not including those in the province of Dauphiné, which will be paid for in addition to the said sum ...

Mousnier, [103], pp. 316–63.

DOCUMENT 18   **HENRY IV'S SPEECH TO THE *PARLEMENT* OF PARIS, 7 FEBRUARY 1599**

In the spring of 1598 the Huguenots were induced, after hard bargaining, to accept the Edict of Nantes. Its implementation, however, met with strong opposition, notably from the parlements. Henry IV had to use all his powers of persuasion. This is how he spoke to members of the Paris Parlement at the Louvre on 7 February 1599.

'Before coming to my reasons for calling you together, I should like to tell you a story of which I have just reminded Marshal La Chastre. Immediately after St Bartholomew's day, four of us who were playing at dice on a table saw some drops of blood appear; we wiped them away twice but they reappeared a third time, after which I refused to go on playing and said it was an augury threatening those who had shed blood. M. de Guise was one of the company.'

After these words His Majesty said what follows: 'You see me here in my study, where I have come to speak to you, not in royal attire like my predecessors, nor with cloak and sword, nor as a prince who has come to speak with foreign ambassadors, but dressed like the father of a family, in a doublet, to speak freely to his children.

What I have to say to you is a request to verify the edict I have granted to the Huguenots. What I have done is in the cause of peace. I have secured peace abroad and I desire peace at home. You are obliged to obey me, if for no other consideration than my rank and the duty all my subjects have towards me, particularly all of you, members of my Parlement. To some I have restored the homes from which they were banished; to others I have given back the faith they had lost. If obedience was due to my predecessors, I can expect even more devotion in that I have established the state; God chose me to set me over this kingdom which is mine both by inheritance and by acquisition. The members of my Parlement would not be in their place but for me. Without wishing to boast I am obliged to say that I have no example to follow but my own. I am aware that there have been intrigues in the Parlement, and preachers urged to talk sedition, but I shall take care of such people without expecting any help from you. That method led straight to the barricades and then by degrees to the late king's assassination. I shall certainly avoid all that kind of thing: I shall nip in the bud all factions and all attempts at seditious preaching; and I shall behead all those who encourage it. I have leapt on to the walls of towns; surely I can leap over barricades, which are not so high.'

Mousnier, [103], pp. 364–5.

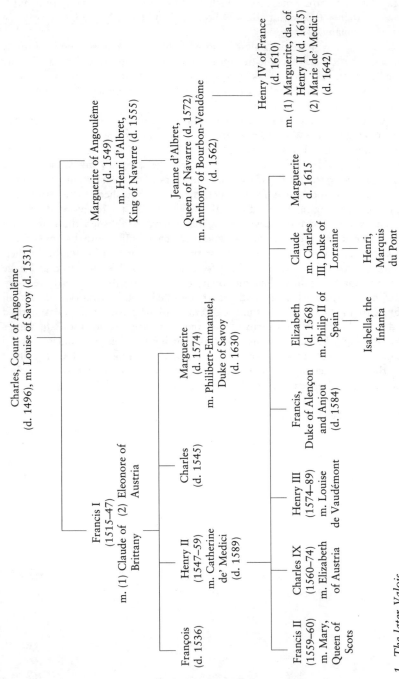

Charles, Count of Angoulême
(d. 1496), m. Louise of Savoy (d. 1531)

Francis I
(1515–47)
m. (1) Claude of (2) Eleonore of
Brittany   Austria

Marguerite of Angoulême
(d. 1549)
m. Henri d'Albret,
King of Navarre (d. 1555)

Jeanne d'Albret,
Queen of Navarre (d. 1572)
m. Anthony of Bourbon-Vendôme
(d. 1562)

Henry IV of France
(d. 1610)
m. (1) Marguerite, da. of
Henry II (d. 1615)
(2) Marie de' Medici
(d. 1642)

François
(d. 1536)

Henry II
(1547–59)
m. Catherine
de' Medici
(d. 1589)

Charles
(d. 1545)

Marguerite
(d. 1574)
m. Philibert-Emmanuel,
Duke of Savoy
(d. 1630)

Francis II
(1559–60)
m. Mary,
Queen of
Scots

Charles IX
(1560–74)
m. Elizabeth
of Austria

Henry III
(1574–89)
m. Louise
de Vaudémont

Francis,
Duke of Alençon
and Anjou
(d. 1584)

Elizabeth
(d. 1568)
m. Philip II of
Spain

Claude
m. Charles
III, Duke of
Lorraine

Marguerite
d. 1615

Isabella, the
Infanta

Henri,
Marquis
du Pont

1. *The later Valois*

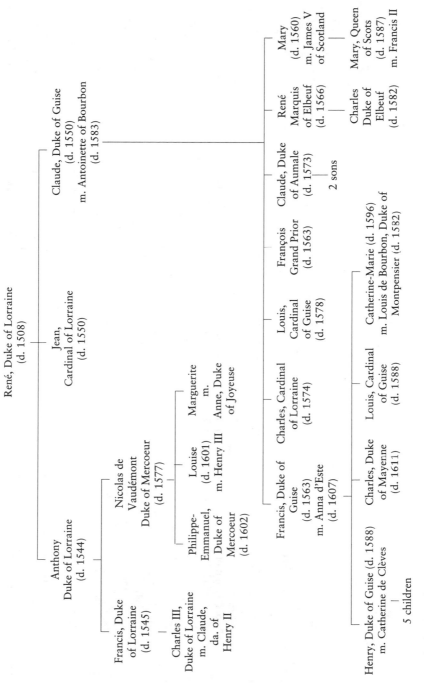

2. *The house of Guise-Lorraine*

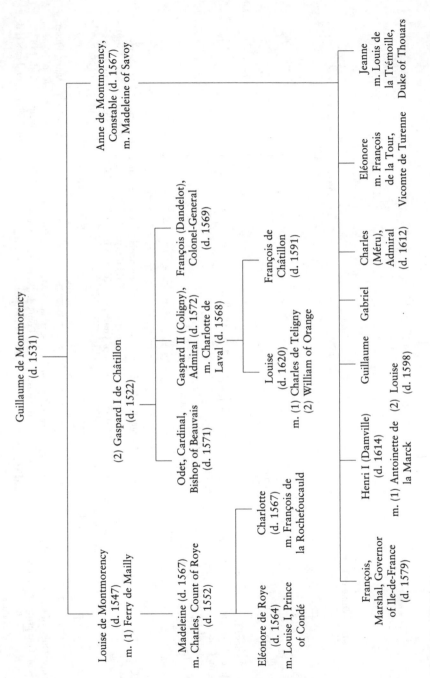

3. *The house of Montmorency*

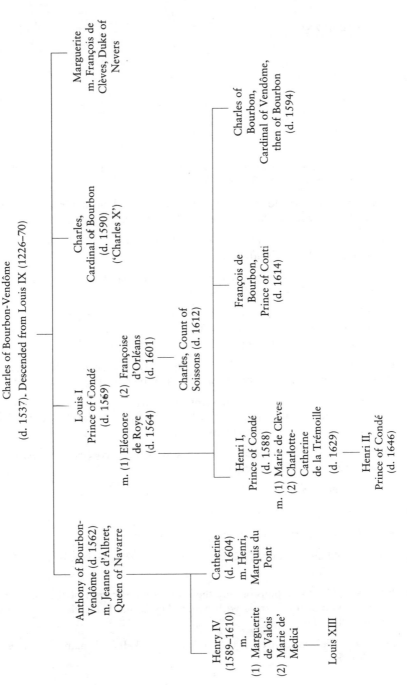

Charles of Bourbon-Vendôme
(d. 1537). Descended from Louis IX (1226–70)

Marguerite
m. François de
Clèves, Duke of
Nevers

Charles,
Cardinal of Bourbon
(d. 1590)
('Charles X')

Charles of
Bourbon,
Cardinal of Vendôme,
then of Bourbon
(d. 1594)

Louis I
Prince of Condé
(d. 1569)

m. (1) Eléonore   (2) Françoise
de Roye   d'Orléans
(d. 1564)   (d. 1601)

Charles, Count of
Soissons (d. 1612)

François de
Bourbon,
Prince of Conti
(d. 1614)

Henri I,
Prince of Condé
(d. 1588)
m. (1) Marie de Clèves
(2) Charlotte-
Catherine
de la Trémoille
(d. 1629)

Henri II,
Prince of Condé
(d. 1646)

Anthony of Bourbon-
Vendôme (d. 1562)
m. Jeanne d'Albret,
Queen of Navarre

Catherine
(d. 1604)
m. Henri,
Marquis du
Pont

Henry IV
(1589–1610)
m.
(1) Marguerite
de Valois
(2) Marie de'
Medici

Louis XIII

4. *The house of Bourbon-Vendôme*

GLOSSARY

Alternatif   The system of selling one office to two persons, each of whom performed its duties for six months.

Arquebus   An early form of portable firearm used on a forked rest. An arquebusier was an infantryman armed with such a weapon.

Bailliage   The basic unit of royal administration at the local level, administered by the *bailli*.

Chambre ardente   The popular name for the chamber of the *parlement* created in 1547 to try cases of heresy.

Chambre mi-partie   A chamber within a *parlement*, comprising an equal number of Catholic and Protestant judges, who were to try cases between members of the two religions. Also called *chambre de l'édit*.

Compagnies d'ordonnance   The armoured cavalry of *gens d'armes* (hence its other name, *gendarmerie*) in which the nobility of the sword served.

Confession of Augsburg   A statement of Lutheran beliefs presented to the German Diet of Augsburg in 1530. Its chief author, Melanchthon, tried to be conciliatory in his phraseology.

Conseil privé   The king's council (also called *conseil des parties*), specialising in judicial business.

Curé   A parish priest.

Droit annuel   Another name for the *Paulette*.

Échevin   An alderman in a municipal government.

Écu   A gold crown. In 1515 it was worth 36 *sous* 3 *deniers*, or about four English shillings.

Élections   Courts responsible for the local administration of the *taille* and other taxes; also the areas with which they dealt. The officials in charge were called *élus*.

Épargne   The central treasury, founded in 1523. Its full name was *Trésor de l'Épargne*.

Estates-General (*États-généraux*)   The national representative body, comprising elected representatives of the three orders of clergy, nobility and third estate. During the Wars of Religion they met in 1560–61, 1561, 1576–77, 1588–89 and 1593.

États particuliers   Representative assemblies held in a few regions within the *pays d'états*.

Gentilhomme campagnard   A member of the rural nobility.

Gouvernement   A provincial governorship.

Grand Conseil   A judicial offshoot of the king's council. It became an independent sovereign court in 1497, but continued to follow the king on his travels.

Grand Parti   A syndicate of Lyons bankers formed in 1555 to consolidate royal debts by means of regular amortisement.

Landsknechts   German mercenary infantry.

Lieutenant criminel   A local magistrate serving in the court of a *bailliage*.

Lieutenant-général du royaume   A title conferring general command of the kingdom. It was given in 1557 to Francis, duke of Guise; in 1561 to Anthony of Bourbon; and in 1588 to Henry, duke of Guise. During the League the duke of Mayenne became *Lieutenant-général* of the state and Crown of France.

Livre   The principal money of account in sixteenth-century France. 1 *livre* = 20 *sous*; 1 *sou* = 12 *deniers*; worth about two English shillings.

Mignon   A term of abuse, implying effeminacy, for one of Henry III's favourites. It may be translated as 'pet' or 'darling'.

Office   A permanent government post (as distinct from a commission, which was temporary). It was often sold and entailed a measure of ennoblement.

Ordinance (*Ordonnance*)   A law or edict.

Parlement   The highest court of law under the king, also responsible for registering royal edicts and with administrative duties. Apart from the *Parlement* of Paris, there were seven provincial *parlements* (Aix-en-Provence, Bordeaux, Dijon, Grenoble, Rennes, Rouen and Toulouse).

Parlementaire   A magistrate serving in a *parlement*.

Parvis   The open space in front of a church: e.g. the *parvis* of Notre-Dame in Paris.

Paulette   A tax upon venal office created in 1604, which gave security to office-holders and their heirs.

Place de sûreté   A fortified town which the Protestants were allowed to garrison. Under the Peace of St Germain (1570) they obtained four such towns (La Rochelle, Cognac, La Charité and Montauban) for two years. The number was raised to eight in the Peace of Monsieur (1576) and to about 100 in the Edict of Nantes (1598).

Police   In sixteenth-century France this meant more than just keeping the peace. It referred to all established administrative procedures.

Politique   A moderate during the civil wars, who was equally opposed to Protestant or Catholic extremism and supported the Crown.

Présidiaux   Courts set up in 1552 between the provincial *parlements* and the *bailliage* courts.

Prévôt des marchands   The Mayor of Paris.

Procureur   A solicitor. In every royal court there was a *procureur du roi*, known in the *parlement* as the *procureur-général*.

Provincial Estates (États provinciaux)   Assemblies of elected representatives of the three estates – nobility, clergy and third estate – which met in a number of provinces, called *pays d'états* (e.g. Brittany, Burgundy, Languedoc and Provence). They were called by the king and met usually once a year.

Reiters   German mercenary cavalry, usually armed with pistols.

Rente   A government bond issued on the security of municipal revenues. A *rentier* was a person living off such an investment.

Sacramentarianism   A body of Protestant thought, held mainly by Zwingli and his followers, which rejected the doctrine of the Real Presence of Christ in the Eucharist.

Salic law   One of the so-called fundamental laws of the French monarchy, whereby females were excluded from the succession to the throne.

Sea Beggars   Dutch Calvinist rebels against Spain who operated mainly at sea.

Seigneurie   The basic economic unit in rural France. The obligation of tenants to the *seigneur* involved a complex of rights, services and dues. A *seigneur* enjoyed rights of jurisdiction of varying degrees (called 'high', 'middle' and 'low') within his lands, albeit subject to appeal to a royal court.

Sénéchaussée   Another name, used mainly in southern France, for a *bailliage*. The equivalent of the *bailli* was the *sénéchal*.

Setier   A measure of capacity.

Sorbonne   The Faculty of Theology of the University of Paris.

Surintendant des finances   The minister responsible for the general supervision of the fiscal system. O was appointed in 1578.

Taille   The principal direct tax, levied in two ways: the *taille personnelle*, levied on the unprivileged in the north, and the *taille réelle*, levied on non-noble land in the south.

Valet de chambre   A title conferring membership of the king's household. It was often purely honorific and entailed no domestic duties.

Vicomté   In local government a jurisdiction below the *bailliage* and equivalent to a *prévôté*.

BIBLIOGRAPHY

Readers should note that several numbers in the bibliography are followed by the letter a, these are books and articles which have been published since this book has gone to press.

PRIMARY SOURCES: MANUSCRIPT

1   Chantilly: Musée Condé. Papiers de Condé. Série L. vol. XIX.

PRIMARY SOURCES: PRINTED

2   Baum, G. and Cunitz, E. (eds), *Histoire ecclésiastique des églises réformées au royaume de France*, 3 vols. Paris, 1833–89.
3   Bodin, Jean, *On Sovereignty*, ed. J.H. Franklin. Cambridge: Cambridge University Press, 1992.
4   Brutus, Stephanus Junius, the Celt, *Vindiciae, contra tyrannos: or, concerning the legitimate power of a prince over the people and of the people over a prince*, ed. and trans. G. Garnett. Cambridge: Cambridge University Press, 1994.
5   Cromé, F., *Dialogue d'entre le maheustre et le manant*, ed. P.M. Ascoli. Geneva: Droz, 1977.
6   De Bèze, Théodore, *Du droit des magistrats*, ed. R.M. Kingdon. Geneva: Droz, 1971.
7   Franklin, J. H., *Constitutionalism and Resistance in the Sixteenth Century: Three Treatises by Hotman, Beza and Mornay*. New York: Pegasus, 1969.
8   Haag, E. and E., *La France Protestante*, 10 vols. Paris, 1846–59. 2nd edn, incomplete, 6 vols. Paris, 1877–88.
9   Haton, C., *Mémoires contenant le récit des événements accomplis de 1553 à 1582*, ed. F. Bourquelot, 2 vols. Paris, 1857.
10   Hotman, F., *Francogallia* ed. R.E. Giesey and J.H.M. Salmon, Cambridge: Cambridge University Press, 1972.
11   La Noue, F. de, *Discours politiques et militaires*, ed. F.E. Sutcliffe. Geneva: Droz, 1967.
12   L'Estoile, Pierre de, *Journal de l'Estoile pour le règne de Henri III (1574–1589)*, ed. L.-R. Lefèvre. Paris: Gallimard, 1943.

13   L'Hospital, Michel de, *Oeuvres complètes*, ed. P.J.S. Dufey, 3 vols.
      Paris, 1824–25.
14   L'Hospital, Michel de, *Discours pour la majorité de Charles IX et
      trois autres discours*, ed. R. Descimon. Paris: Imprimerie nationale,
      1993.
15   Monluc, Blaise de, *Commentaires*, ed. P. Courteault, 3 vols. Paris:
      Picard, 1911.
16   Monluc, Blaise de, *The Valois–Habsburg Wars and the French Wars
      of Religion*, ed. I. Roy. London: Longman, 1971.
17   *The Paris of Henry of Navarre as seen by Pierre de l'Estoile*, ed.
      Nancy L. Roelker. Cambridge, MA: Harvard University Press, 1958.
18   Pasquier, E., *Lettres historiques pour les années 1556–94*, ed. D.
      Thickett. Geneva: Droz, 1966.
19   Stegmann, A., *Édits des Guerres de Religion*. Paris: Vrin, 1979.
20   Tommaseo, N. (ed.), *Relations des ambassadeurs vénitiens sur les
      affaires de France au XVIe siècle*, 2 vols. Paris, 1838.

SECONDARY SOURCES: BOOKS

21   *Actes du colloque L'Admiral de Coligny et son temps*. Paris: Société
      de l'histoire du protestantisme, 1974.
22   Babelon, J.-P., *Henri IV*. Paris: Fayard, 1982.
23   Babelon, J.-P., *Nouvelle histoire de Paris: Paris au XVI siècle*. Paris:
      Hachette, 1986.
24   Barbiche, B., *Sully*. Paris: Albin Michel, 1978.
25   Barnavi, E., *Le Parti de Dieu: Étude sociale et politique des chefs de
      la Ligue parisienne (1585–1594)*. Louvain: Nauwelaerts, 1980.
26   Barnavi, E. and Descimon, R., *La Sainte Ligue, le juge et la potence*.
      Paris: Hachette, 1985.
27   Baumgartner, F.J., *Radical Reactionaries: The Political Thought of
      the French Catholic League*. Geneva: Droz, 1975.
28   Baumgartner, F.J., *Change and Continuity in the French Episcopate:
      The Bishops and the Wars of Religion, 1547–1610*. Durham, NC:
      Duke University Press, 1986.
29   Baumgartner, F.J., *Henry II King of France, 1547–1559*. Durham,
      NC: Duke University Press, 1988.
30   Benedict, P., *Rouen during the Wars of Religion*. Cambridge:
      Cambridge University Press, 1981.
31   Benedict, P. (ed.) *Cities and Social Change in Early Modern France*.
      London: Unwin Hyman, 1989.
32   Bitton, D., *The French Nobility in Crisis, 1560–1640*. Stanford, CA:
      Stanford University Press, 1969.
33   Bonney, R., *The King's Debts: Finance and Politics in France,
      1589–1661*. Oxford: Clarendon Press, 1981.
34   Boucher, Jacqueline, *La cour de Henri III*. Rennes: Ouest-France,
      1986.

35   Bourgeon, J.-L., *L'Assassinat de Coligny*. Geneva: Droz, 1992.
36   Bourquin, L., *Noblesse seconde et pouvoir en Champagne aux XVIe et XVIIe siècles*. Paris: Sorbonne, 1994.
37   Boutier, J., Dewerpe, A. and Nordman, D., *Un tour de France royal: Le voyage de Charles IX (1564–1566)*. Paris: Aubier, 1984.
38   Buisseret, D., *Henry IV*. London: Allen and Unwin, 1984.
39   Buisson, A., *Michel de l'Hospital*. Paris: Hachette, 1950.
40   Cameron, K., *Henri III. A Maligned or Malignant King?* Exeter: University of Exeter, 1978.
41   Cameron, K. (ed.) *From Valois to Bourbon: Dynasty, State and Society in Early Modern France*. Exeter: University of Exeter, 1989.
42   Champion, P., *Catherine de Médicis présente à Charles IX son royaume (1564–1566)*. Paris: Grasset, 1937.
43   Champion, P., *Paris au temps des Guerres de Religion*. Paris: Calmann-Lévy, 1938.
44   Chaunu, P. and Gascon, P., *Histoire économique et sociale de la France: 1450–1660: L'État et la Ville*. Paris: Presses Universitaires de France, 1977.
45   Chevallier, P., *Henri III, roi shakespearien*. Paris: Fayard, 1985.
46   Church, W.F., *Constitutional Thought in Sixteenth-Century France: A Study in the Evolution of Ideas*. Cambridge, MA: Harvard University Press, 1941.
47   Cloulas, I., *Catherine de Médicis*. Paris: Fayard, 1979.
48   Cloulas, I., *Henri II*. Paris: Fayard, 1985.
49   Constant, J.-M., *Les Guise*. Paris: Hachette, 1984.
50   Constant, J.-M., *De la noblesse française aux XVIe–XVIIe siècles*. Paris: Hachette, 1985.
51   Crouzet, D., *Les Guerriers de Dieu*, 2 vols. Paris: Champ Vallon, 1990.
52   Crouzet, D., *La nuit de la Saint-Barthélemy: un rêve perdu de la Renaissance*. Paris: Fayard, 1994.
53   Davis, Natalie Zemon, *Society and Culture in Early Modern France*. London: Duckworth, 1975.
54   Decrue, F., *Anne de Montmorency*. Paris: Plon, 1889.
55   Descimon, R., *Qui étaient les Seize? Mythes et réalités de la Ligue parisienne (1585–1594)*. Paris: Fédération Paris et Île-de-France, 1983.
56   Dewald, J., *The Formation of a Provincial Nobility: The Magistrates of the Parlement of Rouen, 1499–1610*. Princeton, NJ: Princeton University Press, 1980.
57   Diefendorf, Barbara B., *Beneath the Cross: Catholics and Huguenots in Sixteenth-Century Paris*. New York and Oxford: Oxford University Press, 1991.
58   Drouot, H., *Mayenne et la Bourgogne*, 2 vols. Dijon, 1937.
59   Duby, G. (ed.), *Histoire de la France rurale*, Vol. 2. Paris: Seuil, 1975.
60   Duby, G. (ed.), *Histoire de la France urbaine*, Vol. 3. Paris: Seuil, 1981.

61   Evennett, H. Outram, *The Cardinal of Lorraine and the Council of Trent*. Cambridge: Cambridge University Press, 1930.
62   Foisil, Madeleine, *Le Sire de Gouberville*. Paris: Aubier, 1981.
63   Forneron, H., *Les ducs de Guise et leur époque*, 2 vols. Paris: Plon, 1893.
64   Franklin, J.H., *Jean Bodin and the Rise of the Absolutist Theory*. Cambridge: Cambridge University Press, 1973.
65   Garrisson, Janine, *Protestants du Midi (1559–1598)*. Toulouse: Privat, 1981.
66   Garrisson, Janine, *Henry IV*. Paris: Seuil, 1984.
67   Garrisson, Janine, *L'Edit de Nantes et sa révocation. Histoire d'une intolérance*. Paris: Seuil, 1985.
68   Garrisson, Janine, *La Saint-Barthélemy*. Brussels: Complexe, 1987.
69   Garrisson, Janine, *Guerre civile et compromis, 1559–1598*. Paris: Seuil, 1991.
70   Garrisson, Janine, *Marguerite de Valois*. Paris: Fayard, 1994.
70a Garrisson, Janine, *A History of Sixteenth-Century France, 1483– 1598: Renaissance, Reformation and Rebellion*. London: Macmillan, 1995.
71   Gascon, R., *Grand commerce et vie urbaine au XVIe siècle*, 2 vols. Paris: SEVPEN, 1971.
72   Greengrass, M., *The French Reformation*. Oxford: Blackwell, 1987.
73   Greengrass, M., *France in the Age of Henry IV*, 2nd edn. London: Longman, 1995.
74   Harding, R.R., *Anatomy of a Power Elite: The Provincial Governors of Early Modern France*. New Haven, CT: Yale University Press, 1978.
75   Hauser, H., *Études sur la réforme française*. Paris: Picard, 1909.
76   Heller, H., *The Conquest of Poverty: The Calvinist Revolt in Sixteenth-Century France*. Leiden: Brill, 1986.
77   Heller, H. *Iron and Blood: Civil Wars in Sixteenth-Century France*. Montreal and Kingston: McGill-Queen's University Press, 1991.
78   Holt, M.P., *The Duke of Anjou and the Politique Struggle during the Wars of Religion*. Cambridge: Cambridge University Press, 1986.
79   Holt, M.P., (ed.) *Society and Institutions in Early Modern France*. Athens and London: University of Georgia Press, 1991.
79a Holt, M.P. *The French Wars of Religion, 1562–1629*. Cambridge: Cambridge University Press, 1995.
80   Huppert, G., *Les Bourgeois Gentilshommes*. Chicago, IL: University of Chicago Press, 1977.
81   Jacquart, J., *La crise rurale en Île-de-France (1550–1670)*. Paris: SEVPEN, 1974.
82   Jensen, De Lamar, *Diplomacy and Dogmatism: Bernardino de Mendoza and the French Catholic League*. Cambridge, MA: Harvard University Press, 1964.
83   Jouanna, Arlette, *Le devoir de révolte: La noblesse française et la gestation de l'État moderne, 1559–1661*. Paris: Fayard, 1989.

84   Kaiser, W., *Marseille au temps des troubles, 1559–1596: Morphologie sociale et luttes de factions.* Paris: École des Hautes Études en Sciences Sociales, 1991.

85   Kelley, D. R., *François Hotman: A Revolutionary's Ordeal.* Princeton, NJ: Princeton University Press, 1973.

86   Kelley, D. R., *The Beginning of Ideology.* Cambridge: Cambridge University Press, 1981.

87   Kingdon, R. M., *Geneva and the Coming of the Wars of Religion in France, 1555–1563.* Geneva: Droz, 1956.

88   Kingdon, R. M., *Church and Society in Reformation Europe.* London: Variorum Reprints, 1985.

89   Kingdon, R.M., *Myths about the St Bartholomew's Day Massacres, 1572–1576.* Cambridge, MA: Harvard University Press, 1988.

90   Knecht, R.J., *Renaissance Warrior and Patron: The Reign of Francis I.* Cambridge: Cambridge University Press, 1994.

91   Knecht, R.J., *French Renaissance Monarchy: Francis I and Henry II,* 2nd edn. London: Longman, 1996.

92   Knecht, R.J., *The Rise and Fall of Renaissance France.* London: HarperCollins, 1996

93   Lebigre, Arlette, *La révolution des curés: Paris 1588–1594.* Paris: A. Michel, 1980.

94   Lefèvre, L.-R., *Le Tumulte d'Amboise.* Paris: Gallimard, 1949.

95   Le Roy Ladurie, E., *Les paysans de Languedoc,* 2 vols. Paris: SEVPEN, 1966.

96   Le Roy Ladurie, E., *Carnival: A People's Uprising at Romans, (1579–1580).* London: Scolar Press, 1980.

97   Livet, G., *Les guerres de religion.* Paris: Presses Universitaires de France, 1962.

98   Lloyd, H.A., *The State, France, and the Sixteenth Century.* London: Allen & Unwin, 1983.

99   Major, J. Russell, *Representative Government in Early Modern France.* New Haven, CT: Yale University Press, 1980.

100 Major, J. Russell, *From Renaissance Monarchy to Absolute Monarchy: French Kings, Nobles and Estates.* Baltimore, MD and London: John Hopkins University Press, 1994.

101 Mariéjol, J.-H., *La Réforme et La Ligue: L'Édit de Nantes (1559–1598)* (reprinted from E. Lavisse, *Histoire de France,* Vol. vi, 1904). Paris: Hachette, 1983.

102 Martin, A. Lynn, *Henry III and the Jesuit Politicians.* Geneva: Droz, 1973.

103 Mousnier, R., *The Assassination of Henry IV.* London: Faber and Faber, 1973.

104 Neale, J.E., *The Age of Catherine de Medici.* London: Cape, 1943.

105 Neuschel, K., *Word of Honor: Interpreting Noble Culture in Sixteenth-Century France.* Ithaca, NY: Cornell University Press, 1989.

106   Nugent, D., *Ecumenism in the Age of the Reformation: The Colloquy of Poissy*. Cambridge, MA: Harvard University Press, 1974.
107   Nicholls, D., 'France', in *The Early Reformation in Europe*, ed. A. Pettegree. Cambridge: Cambridge University Press, 1992, pp. 120–41.
108   Orléa, M., *La Noblesse aux États généraux de 1576 et de 1588*. Paris: Presses Universitaires de France, 1980.
109   Pallier, D., *Recherches sur l'imprimerie à Paris pendant la Ligue, 1585–1594*. Geneva: Droz, 1976.
110   Parker, T.H.L., *John Calvin*. London: Dent, 1975.
111   Pernot, M., *Les guerres de religion en France, 1559–1598*. Paris: SEDES, 1987.
112   Potter, G. R. and Greengrass, M., *John Calvin*. London: Edward Arnold, 1983.
113   Prestwich, Menna (ed.), *International Calvinism, 1541–1715*. Oxford: Clarendon Press, 1985.
113a Roberts, P., *A city in conflict: Troyes during the French Wars of Religion*, Manchester, Manchester University Press, 1996.
114   Roelker, Nancy L., *Queen of Navarre: Jeanne d'Albret, 1528–1572*. Cambridge, MA: Harvard University Press, 1968.
115   Romier, L., *Les origines politiques des guerres de religion*, 2 vols. Paris, 1913–14.
116   Romier, L., *Le royaume de Catherine de Médicis*, 2 vols. Paris: Perrin, 1922.
117   Romier, L., *La Conjuration d'Amboise*. Paris: Perrin, 1923.
118   Romier, L., *Catholiques et Huguenots à la cour de Charles IX*. Paris: Perrin, 1924.
119   Salmon, J.H.M., *Society in Crisis: France in the Sixteenth Century*. London: Benn, 1975.
120   Salmon, J.H.M., *Renaissance and Revolt: Essays in the Intellectual and Social History of Early Modern France*. Cambridge: Cambridge University Press, 1987.
121   Sauzet, R. (ed.), *Henri III et son temps*. Paris: Vrin, 1992.
122   Sealy, R.J., *The Palace Academy of Henry III*. Geneva: Droz, 1981.
123   Shimizu, J., *Conflict of Loyalties: Politics and Religion in the Career of Gaspard de Coligny, Admiral of France, 1519–1572*. Geneva: Droz, 1970.
124   Skinner, Q., *The Foundations of Modern Political Thought*, 2 vols. Cambridge: Cambridge University Press, 1978.
125   Soman, A. (ed.), *The Massacre of St Bartholomew*. The Hague: M. Nijhoff, 1974.
126   Sutherland, N.M., *The Massacre of St Bartholomew and the European Conflict, 1559–1572*. London: Macmillan, 1973.
127   Sutherland, N.M., *The Huguenot Struggle for Recognition*. New Haven, CT: Yale University Press, 1980.
128   Sutherland, N.M., *Princes, Politics and Religion, 1547–1589*. London: Hambledon, 1984.

129   Wendel, F., *Calvin*. London: Collins, 1965.
130   Wolfe, M., *The Fiscal System of Renaissance France*. New Haven, CT: Yale University Press, 1972.
131   Wolfe, M., *The Conversion of Henri IV: Politics, Power and Religious Belief in Early Modern France*. Cambridge, MA: Harvard University Press, 1993.
132   Wood, J.B., *The Nobility of the Election of Bayeux, 1463–1666: Continuity Through Change*. Princeton, NJ: Princeton University Press, 1980.
133   Yardeni, Myriam, *La Conscience nationale en France pendant les Guerres de Religion (1559–1598)*. Paris: Nauwelaerts, 1971.
134   Yates, Frances A., *The Valois Tapestries*, 2nd edn. London: Routledge and Kegan Paul, 1975.
135   Yates, Frances A., *The French Academies of the Sixteenth Century*. London and New York: Routledge, 1988.

ARTICLES

The following abbreviations are used:

A	*Annales, Économies, Sociétés, Civilisations*
AHR	*American Historical Review*
AR	*Archiv für Reformationsgeschichte*
BEC	*Bibliothèque de l'École des Chartes*
BSHPF	*Bulletin de la Société de l'histoire du Protestantisme Français*
EHR	*English Historical Review*
EHQ	*European History Quarterly*
ESQ	*European Studies Quarterly*
ESR	*European Studies Review*
FH	*French History*
FHS	*French Historical Studies*
H	*History*
HES	*Histoire, économies, sociétés*
HJ	*Historical Journal*
JEH	*Journal of Ecclesiastical History*
JMH	*Journal of Modern History*
PHS	*Proceedings of the Huguenot Society*
P & P	*Past and Present*
RHMC	*Revue d'histoire moderne et contemporaine*
RS	*Renaissance Studies*
SCJ	*Sixteenth Century Journal*

136   Ascoli, P., 'A radical pamphlet of late 16th century France: *le dialogue d'entre le maheustre et le manant*', *SCJ*, v (1974), 3–22.
137   Baumgartner, F.J., 'The case for Charles X', *SCJ*, iv (1973), 87–98.

138 Benedict, P., 'Catholics and Huguenots in sixteenth-century Rouen: the demographic effects of the religious wars', *FHS*, ix (1975), 209–34.

139 Benedict, P., 'The St Bartholomew's massacres in the provinces', *HJ*, xxi (1978), 201–25.

140 Bergin, J., 'The Guises and their benefices, 1588–1641', *EHR*, xcix (1984), 34–58.

141 Bourgeon, J.-L., 'Les légendes ont la vie dure: à propos de la Saint-Barthélemy et de quelques livres récents', *RHMC*, 34 (1987), 102–16.

142 Bourgeon, J.-L., 'Une source sur la Saint-Barthélemy: "l'Histoire de Monsieur de Thou", relue et décryptée', *BSHPF*, 134 (1988), 499–537.

143 Bourgeon, J.-L., 'Pour une histoire, enfin, de la Saint-Barthélemy', *RH*, 282 (1989), 83–142.

144 Bourgeon, J.-L., 'La Fronde parlementaire à la veille de la Saint-Barthélemy', *BEC*, 148 (1990), 17–89.

144a Carroll, S., 'The Guise affinity: popular protest during the Wars of Religion', *FH*, 9 (1995), 125–152.

145 Cooper, R., 'The aftermath of the Blois assassinations of 1588: documents in the Vatican', *FH*, 3 (1989), 404–26.

146 Crouzet, D., 'Recherches sur la crise de l'aristocratie en France au XVIe siècle: les dettes de la maison de Nevers', *HES*, i (1982), 7–50.

147 Crouzet, D., 'Recherches sur les processions blanches, 1583–84', *HES*, 1 (1982), 511–63.

148 Crouzet, D., 'La représentation du temps à l'époque de la Ligue', *RH*, 270 (1984), 297–388.

149 Davies, J.M., 'Persecution and Protestantism: Toulouse, 1562–1575', *HJ*, xxii (1979), 31–51.

150 Davies, J.M., 'Neither politique nor patriot? Henri, duc de Montmorency and Philip II, 1582–1589', *HJ*, 34 (1991), 539–66.

151 Davies, Joan, 'The politics of the marriage bed: matrimony and the Montmorency family, 1527–1612', *FH*, 6 (1992), 63–95.

152 Descimon, R., 'La Ligue à Paris (1585–1594); une révision', *A*, xxxvii (1982), 72–111.

153 Diefendorf, Barbara B., 'Simon Vigor: a radical preacher in sixteenth-century Paris', *SCJ*, 18 (1987), 399–410.

154 Goubert, P., 'Recent theories and research on French population between 1500–1700', in D.V. Glass and D.E.C. Eversley (eds), *Population in History*. London: Edward Arnold, 1965, 456–73.

155 Greengrass, M., 'The anatomy of a religious riot in Toulouse in May 1562', *JEH*, 34 (1983), 469–96.

156 Greengrass, M., 'The *Sainte Union* in the provinces: the case of Toulouse', *SCJ*, xiv (1983), 469–96.

157 Greengrass, M., 'The Sixteen: radical politics in Paris during the League', *H*, 69 (1984), 432–9.

158 Greengrass, M., 'The later Wars of Religion in the French Midi', in

P. Clark (ed.), *The European Crisis of the 1590s*. London: Allen and Unwin, 1985, 106–34.

159   Greengrass, M., 'Dissension in the Provinces under Henry III, 1574–85', in J.R.L. Highfield and R.M. Jeffs (eds), *The Crown and Local Communities in England and France in the Fifteenth Century*. Gloucester: Sutton, (1986), 162–82.

160   Greengrass, M., 'Noble affinities in early modern France: the case of Henri I de Montmorency, Constable of France', *ESQ*, 16 (1986), 275–311.

161   Greengrass, M., 'Property and politics in sixteenth-century France: the landed fortune of Constable Anne de Montmorency', *FH*, 2 (1988), 371–98.

162   Greengrass, M., 'The psychology of religious violence', *FH*, 5 (1991), 467–74.

163   Harding, R., 'Revolution and reform in the Holy League', *JMH*, 53 (1981), 379–86.

164   Holt, M.P., 'The king in Parlement: the problem of the *lit de justice* in sixteenth-century France', *HJ*, 31 (1988), 507–23.

165   Kettering, Sharon, 'Gift-giving and patronage in early modern France', *FH*, 2 (1988), 131–51.

166   Kettering, Sharon, 'The patronage power of early modern French noblewomen', *HJ*, 32 (1989), 817–41.

167   Kettering, Sharon, 'Friendship and clientage in early modern France', *FH*, 6 (1992), 139–58.

168   Kim, Seong-Hak, 'Michel de l'Hôpital revisited', *Proceedings of the Annual Meeting of the Western Society for French History*, 17 (1990), 106–12.

169   Kim, Seong-Hak, 'The Chancellor's crusade: Michel de l'Hôpital and the *Parlement* of Paris', *FH*, 7 (1993), 1–29.

170   Knecht, R.J., 'Francis I, "Defender of the Faith"?', in E.W. Ives, R.J. Knecht and J.J. Scarisbrick (eds), *Wealth and Power in Tudor England*. London: Athlone, 1978.

171   Knecht, R.J., 'Defending the faith in 16th-century France', *PHS*, 26 (1994), 1–13.

172   Knecht, R.J., 'The sword and the pen: Blaise de Monluc and his *Commentaires*', *RS*, 9 (1995), 104–18.

173   Koenigsberger, H.G., 'The organisation of revolutionary parties in France and the Netherlands during the sixteenth century', *JMH*, 27 (1955), 335–51.

174   Konnert, M., 'Urban values versus religious passion: Châlons-sur-Marne during the Wars of Religion', *SCJ*, 20 (1989), 387–405.

175   Major, J. Russell, 'The crown and the aristocracy in Renaissance France', *AHR*, lxix (1964), 631–45.

176   Major, J. Russell, 'Noble income and inflation and the wars of religion in France', *AHR*, lxxxvi (1981), 21–48.

177 Neely, Sylvia, 'Michel de l'Hospital and the *Traité de la réformation de la justice*: a case of misattribution', *FHS*, 14 (1986), 339–66.

178 Nicholls, D., 'Social change and early protestantism in France: Normandy, 1520–62', *ESR*, x (1980), 279–308.

179 Nicholls, D., 'The social history of the French Reformation: ideology, confession and culture', *Social History*, ix (1984), 25–43.

180 Nicholls, D., 'The theatre of martyrdom in the French Reformation', *P & P*, 121 (1988), 49–73.

181 Nicholls, D., 'Protestants, Catholics and magistrates in Tours, 1562–1572. The making of a Catholic city during the religious wars', *FH*, 8 (1994), 14–33.

182 Potter, D., 'The duc de Guise and the fall of Calais, 1557–1558', *EHR*, 388 (1983), 481–512.

182a Potter, D., 'Kingship in the Wars of Religion: the reputation of Henry III of France', *EHQ*, 25 (1995) 485–528.

183 Potter, D. and Roberts, P.R., 'An Englishman's view of the Court of Henri III, 1584–1585: Richard Cook's – "Description of the Court of France" ', *FH*, 2 (1988), 312–44.

184 Ranum, O., 'The French ritual of tyrannicide in the late sixteenth century', *SCJ*, xi (1980), 63–82.

185 Richet, D., 'Aspects socio-culturels des conflits religieux à Paris dans la seconde moitié du XVIe siècle', *A*, xxxii (1977), 764–89.

186 Roberts, Penny, 'Religious conflict and the urban setting: Troyes during the French Wars of Religion', *FH*, 6 (1992), 259–78.

187 Roelker, Nancy M., 'The role of noblewomen in the French Renaissance', *AR*, 63 (1972), 168–95.

188 Schalk, E., 'The appearance and reality of nobility in France during the wars of religion: an example of how collective attitudes can change', *JMH*, xlviii (1976), 19–31.

189 Wolfe, M., 'Piety and political allegiance: the duc de Nevers and the Protestant Henri IV, 1589 93', *FH*, 2 (1988), 1–21.

INDEX